101
Crazy Quilt
Blocks

by Linda Causee

Bobbie Matela, Managing Editor

Carol Wilson Mansfield, Art Director

Linda Causee, Editorial Director

Christina Wilson, Associate Editor

Wendy Mathson, Editorial Assistant and Graphic Designer

Wendy Mathson and Terea Mitchell, Illustrations

Blocks were foundation-pieced by Linda Causee, Meredith Montross, Carly Poggemeyer, Glenda Tucker, Kathy Wesley and Christina Wilson.

Trimming and embroidery was done by Linda Causee, Carol Wilson Mansfield, Bobbie Matela, Leslie Sowden, Glenda Tucker and Christina Wilson.

Thank you to the following companies who generously supplied products for our blocks:

Bernina® of America: Artista 180 sewing machine

Quilter's Resource: Fabrics, trims and charms

JHB International: Buttons

Wright's®: Lace, trims and appliques

Mill Hill: Ceramic buttons, Glass Treasures and Crystals

For a full-color catalog including books on quilting, write to:

American School of Needlework®
Consumer Division
1455 Linda Vista Drive
San Marcos, CA 92069

e-mail us at: catalog@asnpub.com
visit us at: www.asnpub.com

Introduction

Everyone's crazy for crazy quilts! Here's a wonderful collection of foundation-pieced blocks that will ensure that beginners to this technique will enjoy going crazy on their next quilt, while those who have already acquired the crazy quilt habit will find a treasury of ideas for their crazy quilts.

Along with this collection of 101 full-sized block patterns, we have also included twenty of the most useful decorative embroidery stitches for embellishing seams.

We have used purchased lace, trims, interesting buttons, and charms on our photographed blocks. Our embellishments are only suggestions, as you may want to use mementos and old fabrics and trims that you have collected over the years that have special personal meaning.

101 Crazy Quilt Blocks offers a collection of ideas on how to make as well as embellish crazy quilt blocks. Many of the block patterns have a theme:

Hearts	Blocks 9 and 76
Birdhouses	Blocks 13, 19 and 68
Fans	Blocks 5 and 89
Baskets	Blocks 61, 65, 66 and 81
Wreaths	Blocks 7 and 91
Flowers	Blocks 40, 42, 43, 45, 55 and 62

Use any of the blocks and embellish with a specific theme:

Patriotic	Blocks 53 and 59
Kids	Blocks 35, 36, 51, and 84
Christmas	Blocks 12 and 93
Angels	Blocks 3, 10, 41, and 44
Hearts	Blocks 15, 21, 38, 47, 79, 80 and 97
Sewing	Blocks 4, 32, 39 and 88
Folk Art	Blocks 23, 83 and 94
Celestial/Millennium	Blocks 59 and 101

General Directions

Supplies for Making Crazy Quilts

Fabrics

Crazy quilts can be made from fancy fabrics such as silks, satins, velvets or brocades, as well as wools, cottons, or just about anything that fits into the color scheme and design of your crazy quilt. Use pastels, country colors, jewel tones or darks. Prints as well as solids can be effective. The most important thing to remember is to include a variety of fabrics to achieve a balanced look. If you want to use fancy embroidery stitches, pick fabrics that will show off, not detract from, the embroidery.

Thread and Ribbons

A variety of threads can be used for crazy quilt stitches. Six-strand cotton floss, rayon floss, pearl cotton (size 8), silk buttonhole twist, ribbon floss, and metallics are all suitable. Choose colors that will show off your embroidery to its best advantage: light colors on dark fabrics and dark colors on light fabric. Instructions for the embroidery stitches are on pages 4 to 7.

A minimal amount of embroidery, mainly Colonial Knots and Running Stitches, was done with 4mm silk ribbon.

Needles

Due to the variety of fabrics and threads in crazy quilts, it is best to have several different types and sizes of needles. Crewel, tapestry and chenille needles all work for thread as well as ribbon embroidery. Crewel needles (sizes 6 to 8) or chenille needles (sizes 18 to 24) are best for heavier fabrics, such as velvet, and can be used for ribbon embroidery. Tapestry needles (sizes 24 to 26) are also suitable for ribbon embroidery. If you are adding seed beads to your crazy quilt, beading needles are recommended.

Embellishments

Add a wide assortment of embellishments to your crazy quilt for those special touches. Glass seed beads, pebble beads, crystal beads, buttons, laces, charms—the possibilities are endless. Try using seed beads in place of French or Colonial Knots.

Frames and Hoops

You may choose to use a frame or hoop to hold the fabric taut while you stitch. Select the hoop size most comfortable for you. However, remember to add embellishments after you remove your quilt from the hoop. Otherwise, use a hoop or frame large enough so as not to interfere with embellishments that have already been attached.

Embroidery Stitches

The crazy quilt blocks in this collection have been embellished with several different embroidery stitches. Some are used alone, some are used in combination with others. Instructions for those used in the photographed blocks are given on the next several pages. Many more can be found in *An Encyclopedia of Crazy Quilt Stitches and Motifs*, Book #4178, published by ASN Publishing.

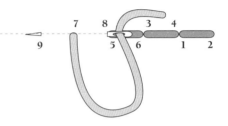

Backstitch

Bring needle up at 1, a stitch length away from beginning of design line. Stitch back down at 2, at beginning of line. Bring needle up at 3, then stitch back down to meet previous stitch at 1. Continue in this manner, stitching backward on surface to meet previous stitch. Backstitch can be worked along curved or straight lines.

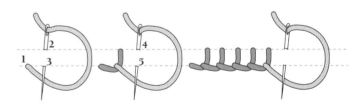

Blanket Stitch

Bring needle up at 1 and reinsert needle at 2 (diagonally to the right of 1). Bring needle up at 3 (down and slightly to left of 2) keeping thread under point of needle. Pull thread through to form stitch. Continue working from left to right keeping stitches the same distance apart and the same height.

Blanket Stitch-Closed

The Closed Blanket Stitch is similar to the regular Blanket Stitch except that the tops of the stitches are worked into the same hole (2) to form a triangular shape. Bring the needle up at 1. Loop thread to the right and insert needle at 2. Bring needle back up at 3, making sure needle goes over loop and pull into place. Go down at 4 (same hole as 2) and come up at 5 to form the triangle. Continue in same manner, working left to right.

Chain Stitch

Bring needle up at 1, form a counterclockwise loop and go down at 2 (same hole as 1), holding loop with left thumb. Come up at 3 bringing the tip of the needle over the loop. Repeat stitch to form a chain. The chain can be worked horizontally, vertically, or along a curve. End chain by making a small stitch over final loop.

Chevron Stitch

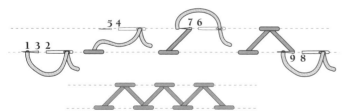

Work Chevron stitch from left to right between two imaginary parallel lines. Use it as a border or filling. Bring needle up at 1, down at 2; hold the thread down with thumb of non-stitching hand, and make a small stitch bringing needle up at 3 (halfway between 1 and 2). Reinsert needle at 4, diagonally above 3, and bring out at 5. Insert needle at 6 keeping thread above needle and bring out at 7 (same hole as 4). Insert at 8 and come up at 9. Continue working stitch in same manner.

Colonial Knot

Come up at 1, make a clockwise loop and slip point of needle beneath thread from left to right. Bring thread around point of needle in a figure eight motion. Insert needle at 2 (next to, but not into 1); pull thread while pulling needle through to back of fabric.

Cretan Stitch

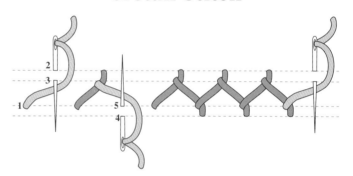

Come up at 1. Go down at 2 (above and to the right of 1) and emerge at 3 (directly below and desired distance from 2) with tip of needle over top of thread. Insert needle at 4 and emerge at 5 (directly above 4 and the same distance as between 2 and 3) with tip of needle over top of thread. Continue working in same manner along pairs of imaginary parallel lines, keeping vertical stitches evenly spaced.

Cross Stitch

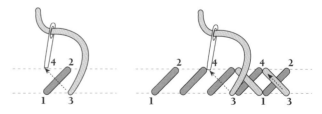

Bring needle up at 1 and down at 2. Complete the stitch by coming up at 3 and down at 4. When doing a row of Cross Stitches, make all stitches from 1 to 2 first; going from left to right. Complete row by working from right to left along two imaginary parallel lines with stitches from bottom right to upper left.

Feather Stitch

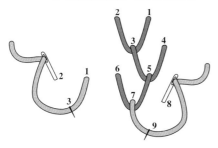

Come up at 1 and go down at 2 (to left of and even with 1); emerge at 3 (below and between 1 and 2) with tip of needle over thread. Pull thread completely through and go down at 4 (to right of and even with 3); emerge at 5 below 3 and 4 and directly under 1). Pull thread completely through and continue stitching in same manner. End by making a small stitch over last loop.

Fly Stitch

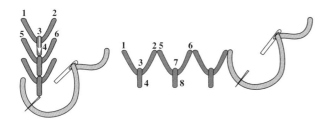

Bring needle up at 1 and down at 2; keep stitch loose. Come up at 3 and pull thread to form a "V"; go down at 4. Continue in same manner going vertically or horizontally.

French Knot

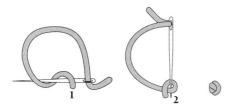

Bring needle up at 1. Wrap thread once around shaft of needle. Insert point of needle at 2 (close to, but not into 1). Hold knot down as you pull needle through to the back of fabric.

Herringbone Stitch

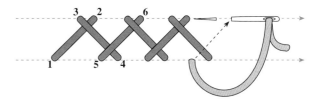

Bring needle up at 1 along an imaginary line. Insert needle at 2, diagonally above 1 and bring up at 3. Reinsert needle at 4 and bring out at 5. Continue in this manner working from left to right. This stitch can be used as a border or filler.

Lazy Daisy Stitch

Bring needle up at 1 and reinsert needle at 2 (same hole as 1). Bring needle up at 3 at desired length of loop, and pull thread until loop is formed. Stitch down over the loop at 4.

Maidenhair Stitch

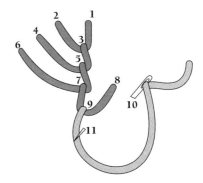

Come up at 1 and down at 2 (to left of and even with 1); emerge at 3 (below and to left of 1) bringing tip of needle over thread. Pull needle through and go down at 4 (to left of and even with 2); emerge at 5 (below and to left of 3). Pull needle through and go down at 6 (to left of and even with 4) and emerge at 7 (below and to left of 5). Pull needle through and go down at 8 (to right and even with 7) and emerge at 9. Continue in same manner for two more stitches, and then do alternating groups of three stitches for desired length.

Running Stitch

Work stitches from right to left. Bring needle up at 1 and down at 2. Continue stitching, keeping length of stitches the same as the spaces between.

Satin Stitch

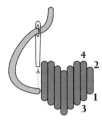

Come up at 1 and down at 2. Continue with Straight Stitches very close together to fill desired pattern.

Stem Stitch

Bring needle up at 1. Hold thread down with thumb of your non-stitching hand. Reinsert needle at 2 and bring up at 3, about halfway between 1 and 2. Pull thread through and continue in this manner with thread held below stitching. Work in straight or curved lines.

Straight Stitch

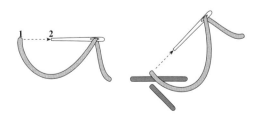

Come up at 1 and down at 2. Straight Stitches can be varying sizes and spaced regularly or irregularly.

Vandyke Stitch

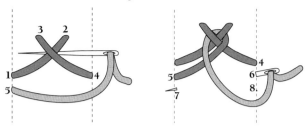

Come up at 1 and down at 1; come back up at 3 (to left of and even with 2) and go down at 4. Come up at 5 (directly below and even with 1) and pass needle under area where threads cross going from right to left. Pull needle through, keeping loop loose. Go down at 6 (directly below and even with 5) and up at 7. Pass needle under previous crossed stitches and go down at 8. Continue in same manner for desired length.

Wheat Ear Stitch

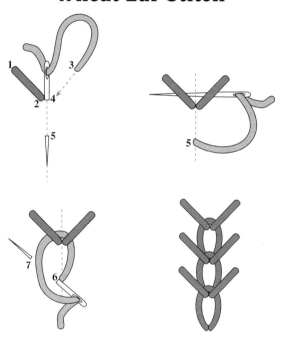

Come up at 1 and down at 2, up at 3 (even with and to right of 1) and down at 4 (same hole as 2). Emerge at 5, directly below 2 and 4 (about same distance as length between 1 and 2 and 3 and 4). Pull needle through completely and loop needle under the two stitches just made going from right to left. Go down at 6 (same hole as 5). Come back up at 7 and continue next stitch in same manner.

Machine Embroidery

If you have access to a sewing machine with embroidery stitches, you may choose to embroider your Crazy Quilt Blocks by machine. Since every machine is different, experiment with yours to sample the various stitches. Use a tear-away stabilizer when doing decorative machine embroidery.

Preparing the Foundation

Crazy quilt patchwork is done on a foundation such as a lightweight cotton, muslin or interfacing. The foundation stabilizes lightweight fabrics like silk, and makes embroidery on those fabrics easier. It also stabilizes the outer edges of the blocks, making grainline considerations unimportant. Another important factor in using a foundation is that it covers the seam allowances of fancy fabrics that tend to fray easily. The foundation will keep them from fraying further while embroidering. Using a paper foundation is not recommended, since it must be removed after sewing.

Tracing the Block

Carefully trace desired block (found on pages 12 to 48, and pages 53 to 116) onto a piece of foundation fabric that is at least 1/4" larger on all sides than the pattern. Use a ruler and fine-point permanent fabric marker or pencil to make straight lines. Be sure to include all numbers, using a light touch on light-colored fabrics so they do not show through.

Hint: If you find it difficult to trace onto fabric, iron a piece of freezer paper (shiny side) to back of fabric first.

Transferring the Block

The block patterns can also be transferred onto foundation fabric using a transfer pen or pencil. This method is preferable if you will be using the same block more than once in your quilt, since you can use a transfer pattern several times. (Refer to manufacturer's directions.) If using this method, you must first reverse the pattern. To do so, trace pattern onto tracing paper using a black marker. Turn paper over so the pattern is face down. You should still be able to see pattern clearly through tracing paper; if not, use a light box or tape it to a sunny window. Trace pattern (not numbers) onto plain paper, using a transfer pen or pencil, **Fig 1**.

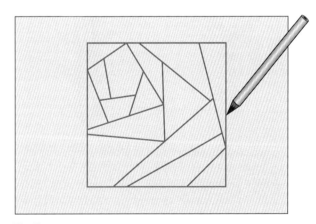

Fig 1

Following manufacturer's directions, iron transfer onto foundation material. Write numbers on foundation with a light touch using a fine-point marking pen or regular lead pencil.

Making a Crazy Quilt Block

*Note: The crazy quilt patterns in this book are not symmetrical. Therefore, when completed, the blocks will appear as mirror images of the patterns, **Fig 2**. Keep this in mind when deciding on fabric placement.*

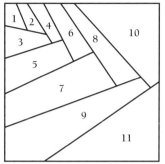

Fig 2

1. Measure and draw a line on foundation 1/4" from outside edges of block, then cut just outside drawn line, **Fig 3**.

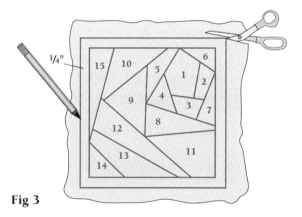

Fig 3

2. Cut a piece of fabric large enough to cover and overlap space #1. Place fabric piece right side up over space #1 on unmarked side of foundation; make sure fabric piece overlaps space by at least 1/4" on all sides, **Fig 4**. Pin in place.

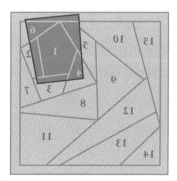

Fig 4

Note: If you cannot see through your foundation, hold it up to a light source to make sure your fabric piece adequately overlaps the marked space.

3. Cut a fabric piece large enough to overlap space #2 by at least ¼" on all sides. Place fabric #2 piece right sides together with first piece, **Fig 5**.

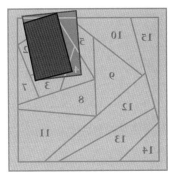

Fig 5

*Note: Double check to see that fabric piece will cover and overlap space #2 adequately by folding it out along line between spaces #1 and #2, **Fig 6**. Fold back to original position.*

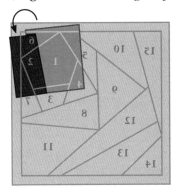

Fig 6

4. Turn foundation with marked side facing you and fold foundation toward you along line between spaces #1 and #2; trim both fabric pieces to about ¼" above fold line, if necessary, **Fig 7**.

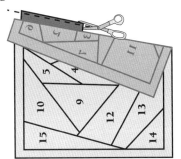

Fig 7

5. With marked side of foundation up, sew along line between spaces #1 and #2, **Fig 8**; begin and end stitching two to three stitches beyond marked lines.

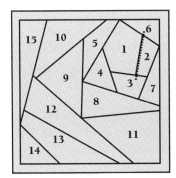

Fig 8

6. Turn foundation over; open piece #2 and finger press seam, **Fig 9**. Pin in place.

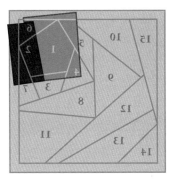

Fig 9

7. Holding foundation with marked side facing you, fold foundation toward you along line between spaces #1/#2, and #3 and trim fabric about ¼" from fold, **Fig 10**.

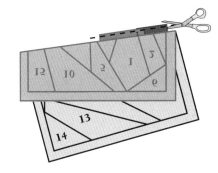

Fig 10

8. Turn foundation with unmarked side up and place fabric #3 right side down, even with just-trimmed edge, **Fig 11**.

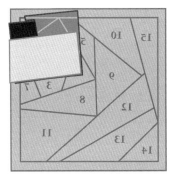

Fig 11

9. Turn foundation to marked side and sew along line between spaces #1/#2 and #3; begin and end sewing two or three stitches beyond line, **Fig 12**.

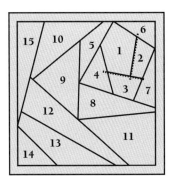

Fig 12

10. Turn foundation over, open out piece #3 and finger press seam, **Fig 13**. Pin in place.

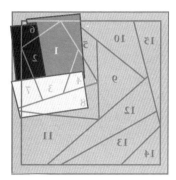

Fig 13

11. Turn foundation with marked side facing you; fold foundation toward you along line between spaces #1/#3 and #4 and trim fabric 1/4" above fold, **Fig 14**.

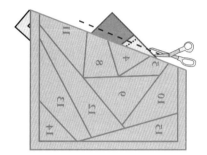

Fig 14

Note: If previous stitching makes it difficult to fold foundation along line, fold it as far as it will go and trim to about 1/4" from marked line.

12. Continue trimming and sewing pieces in numerical order until entire foundation is covered, **Fig 15**. Be sure all pieces along outer edge overlap edge of foundation.

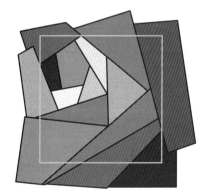

Fig 15

Press stitched foundation with wrong side (foundation side) up. Do not trim outer edges at this time.

13. Stay stitch just outside outer marked edge of block, **Fig 16**.

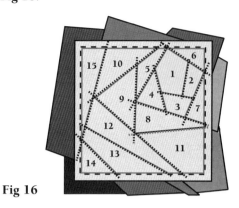

Fig 16

14. Trim outside edges of block to 1/4" from marked line, **Fig 17**.

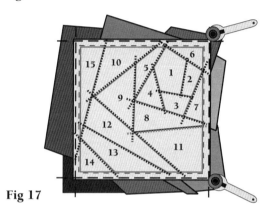

Fig 17

15. Repeat steps 1 to 14 for the number of blocks needed for your project.

16. Add embroidery stitches, laces and embellishments to blocks as desired.

Note: Do not place embellishments too close to edges of blocks.

Finishing Your Quilt
Making the Quilt Top

Lay out blocks in a pleasing arrangement. Sew quilt blocks together in rows; press seams for rows in alternate directions. Sew rows together, matching seams. If making quilt with sashing, lay out blocks and sashing and sew together into rows. Press quilt top carefully, face down on a padded surface.

To add borders, measure quilt top lengthwise; cut two border strips to that length and sew to sides of quilt. Measure quilt top crosswise, including borders just added; cut two border strips to that length. Sew to top and bottom of quilt top. Repeat for any additional borders. Add embellishments to cover seams and corners if desired.

Layering the Quilt

Note: Although traditionally not used, if you would like a filler layer, use a very thin batting, fleece, flannel, or even muslin. Cut the filler the same size as the backing and place between backing and quilt top.

Cut backing fabric (and filler, if used) to extend at least 1/2" beyond edge of quilt top on all four sides. (Piece backing as necessary to make it large enough.) Lay backing fabric wrong side up on a flat surface, then filler; place quilt top right side up, centered on backing.

Baste or pin layers together using one of the following methods.

Thread basting – Baste with long stitches, starting in center and sewing toward edges in a number of diagonal lines.

Safety pin basting – Pin through all layers at once starting from center and working toward edges. Place pins no more than 4" apart, thinking of your quilt plan as you work to make certain pins avoid prospective quilting lines.

Quilt gun basting – Use the handy trigger tool (found in quilt and fabric stores) that pushes nylon tags through all layers of the quilt. Start in center and work randomly toward outside edges. Place tags about 4" apart. You can sew right over the tags and then easily remove them by cutting off with a pair of scissors.

Spray basting – Use one of the spray adhesives currently on the market, following manufacturer's directions.

Tying the Quilt

1. Thread a length of six-strand floss or pearl cotton in a large tapestry needle.

2. Following **Fig 18,** push the needle through the quilt from top to back (1), leaving a short tail; bring needle up a short distance away (2). Go back down (1) and up (2) through original holes.

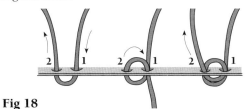

Fig 18

3. Tie ends into a double knot, **Fig. 19,** and trim to 1". Repeat knots at corners and random areas of blocks.

Fig 19

Note: If you do not want loose ends on the front of your quilt, repeat above steps except start from the back and tie knot on back of quilt.

Attaching the Binding

Trim backing and batting even with quilt top. For side edges, measure quilt top lengthwise; cut two 2"-wide strips that length. Fold strips in half lengthwise wrong sides together. Place one strip along one side of the quilt; sew with a 1/4" seam allowance, **Fig 20**.

Fig 20

Turn binding to back and slipstitch to backing covering previous stitching line, **Fig 21**. Repeat on other side.

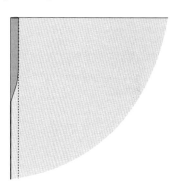

Fig 21

For top and bottom edges, measure quilt crosswise and cut two 2"-wide strips that length, adding 1/2" to each end. Fold strips in half lengthwise with wrong sides together. Place one strip along top edge with 1/2" extending beyond each side; sew with a 1/4" seam allowance, **Fig 22**. Turn binding to back and tuck the extra 1/2" under at each end; slipstitch to backing fabric. Repeat at bottom edge.

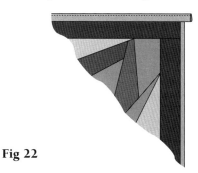

Fig 22

The Finishing Touch

After your quilt is finished, always sign and date it. A label can be cross stitched, embroidered or even written with a permanent marking pen. To make decorative labels in a hurry, *Iron-on Transfers for Quilt Labels* (ASN #4188) and *Foundation-Pieced Quilt Labels* (ASN #4196), provide many patterns for fun and unique quilt labels. Hand stitch to back of quilt.

1

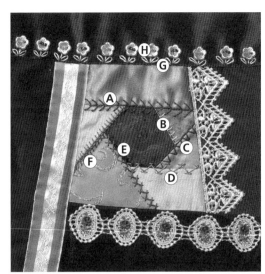

(A) Fly Stitch
(B) Blanket Stitch
(C) Blanket Stitch-closed
(D) Chevron Stitch
(E) Herringbone Stitch
(F) Vandyke Stitch
(G) Lazy Daisy
(H) Straight Stitch

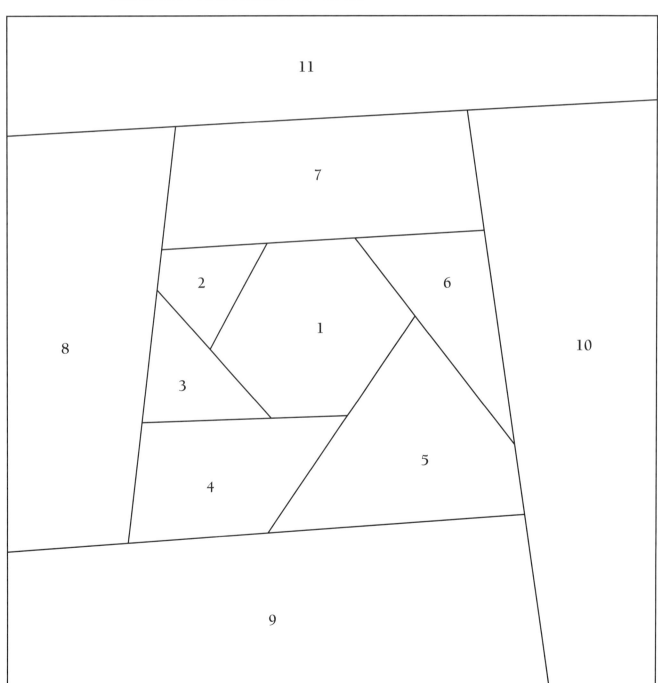

(A) Blanket Stitch
(B) Feather Stitch
(C) Vandyke Stitch
(D) Chevron Stitch
(E) Blanket Stitch-closed
(F) Herringbone Stitch
(G) Cretan Stitch
(H) Wheat Ear Stitch
(I) Straight Stitch
(J) Colonial Knot

2

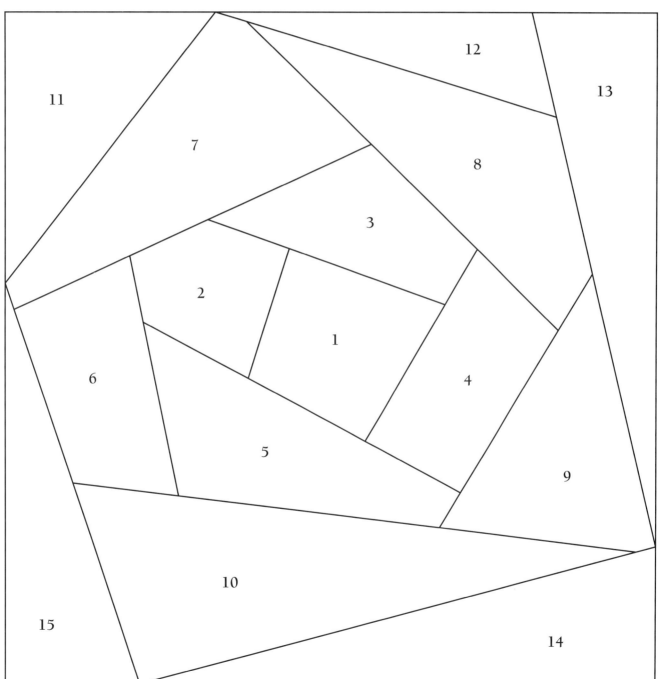

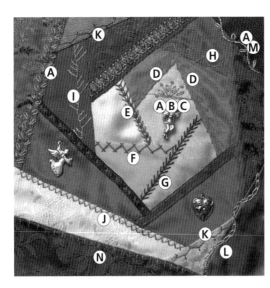

(A) Lazy Daisy
(B) Colonial Knot
(C) Straight Stitch
(D) Feather Stitch
(E) Wheat Ear Stitch
(F) Herringbone Stitch
(G) Fly Stitch
(H) Chevron Stitch
(I) Maidenhair Stitch
(J) Cross Stitch
(K) Cretan Stitch
(L) Chain Stitch
(M) Stem Stitch
(N) Blanket Stitch

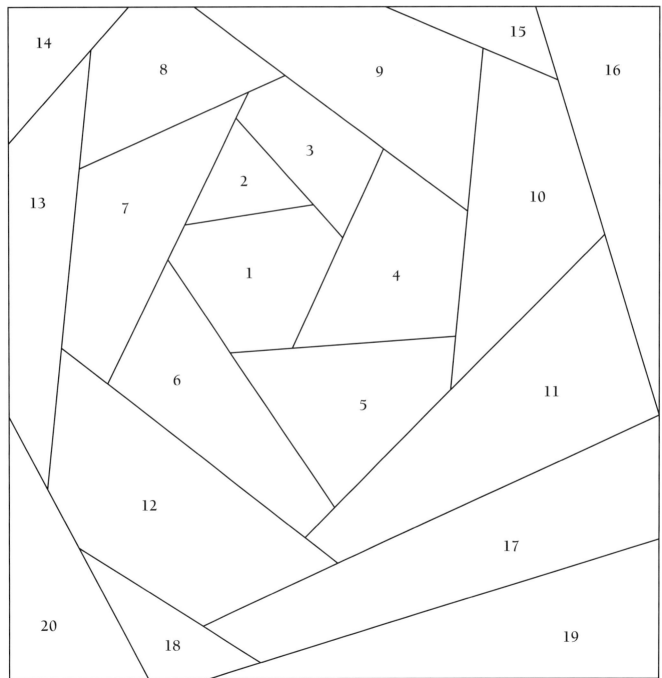

- Ⓐ Cross Stitch
- Ⓑ Fly Stitch
- Ⓒ Blanket Stitch
- Ⓓ Feather Stitch
- Ⓔ Lazy Daisy
- Ⓕ Colonial Knot
- Ⓖ Wheat Ear Stitch
- Ⓗ Herringbone Stitch
- Ⓘ Maidenhair Stitch

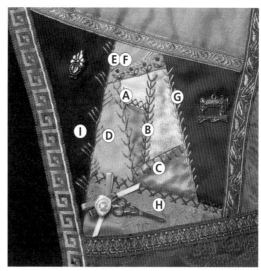

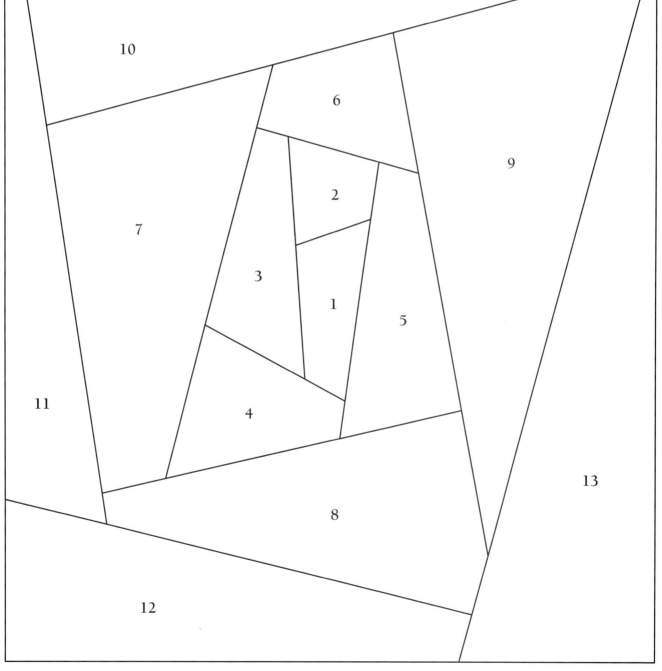

5

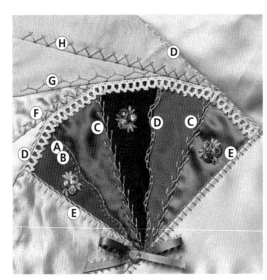

(A) Stem Stitch
(B) French Knot
(C) Feather Stitch
(D) Chain Stitch
(E) Blanket Stitch
(F) Chevron Stitch
(G) Cretan Stitch
(H) Herringbone Stitch

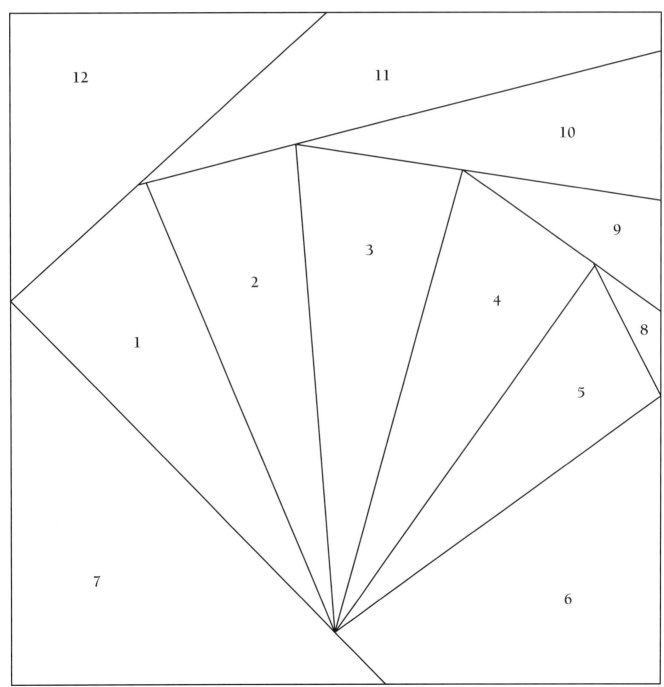

(A) Blanket Stitch
(B) Fly Stitch
(C) Wheat Ear Stitch
(D) Chain Stitch (two rows)
(E) Vandyke Stitch
(F) Cretan Stitch
(G) Feather Stitch
(H) Maidenhair Stitch
(I) Lazy Daisy

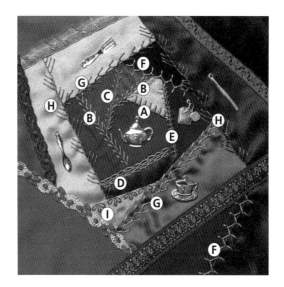

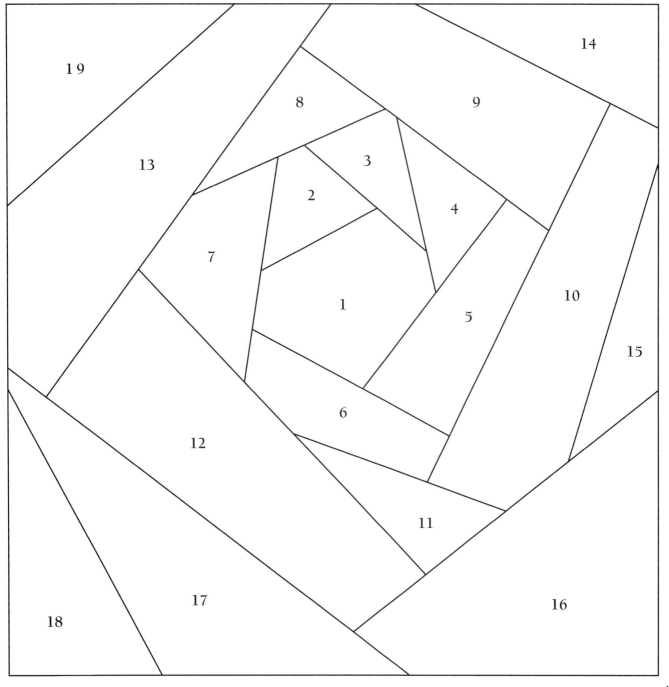

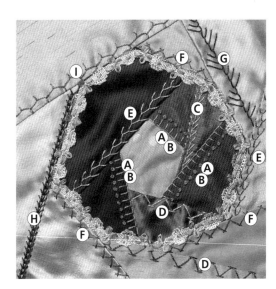

- (A) Blanket Stitch
- (B) Colonial Knot
- (C) Fly Stitch
- (D) Chevron Stitch
- (E) Feather Stitch
- (F) Herringbone Stitch
- (G) Maidenhair Stitch
- (H) Wheat Ear Stitch
- (I) Cretan Stitch

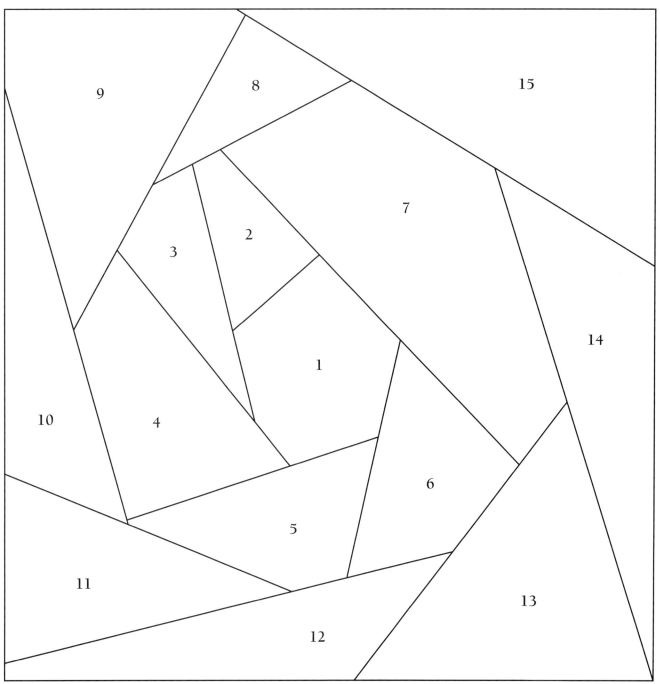

A Blanket Stitch
B Feather Stitch (with beads)
C Stem Stitch
D Colonial Knot
E Fly Stitch
F Wheat Ear Stitch
G Vandyke Stitch

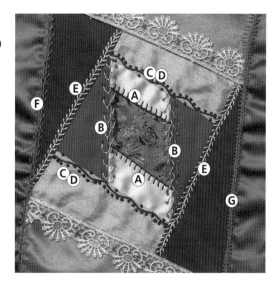

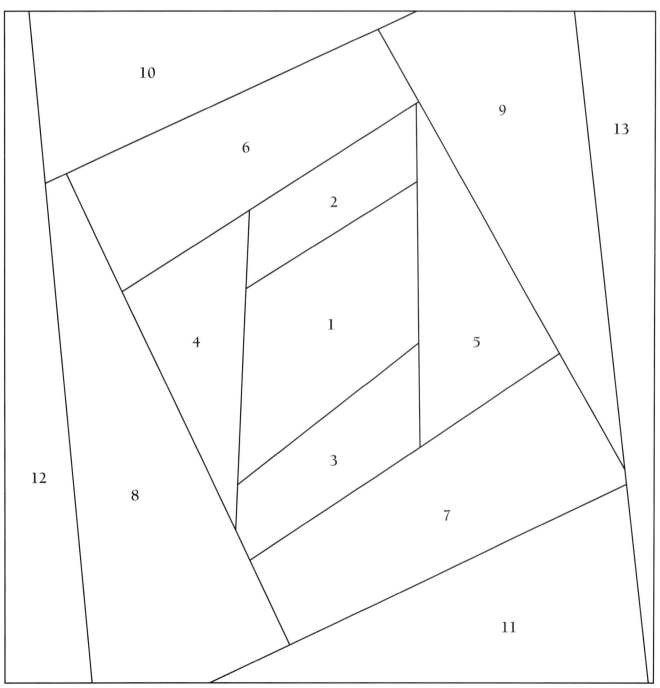

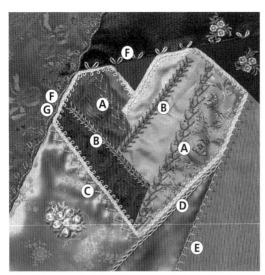

(A) Feather Stitch
(B) Wheat Ear Stitch
(C) Herringbone Stitch
(D) Chain Stitch
(E) Blanket Stitch
(F) Lazy Daisy
(G) Stem Stitch

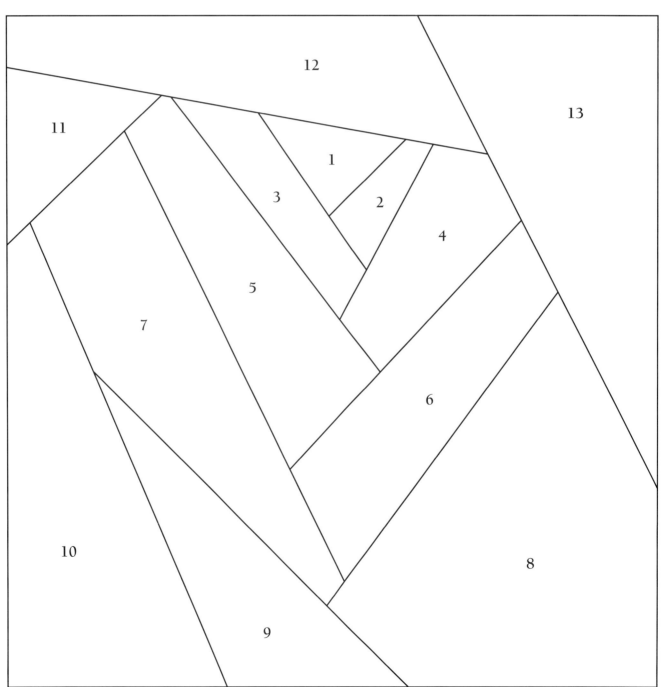

(A) Chain Stitch
(B) Blanket Stitch-closed
(C) Fly Stitch
(D) Feather Stitch
(E) Chevron Stitch
(F) Vandyke Stitch
(G) Cretan Stitch
(H) Wheat Ear Stitch
(I) Herringbone Stitch
(J) Cross Stitch
(K) French Knot

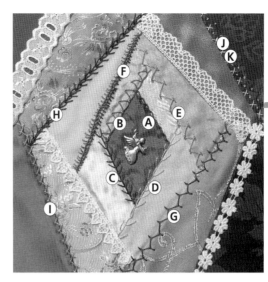

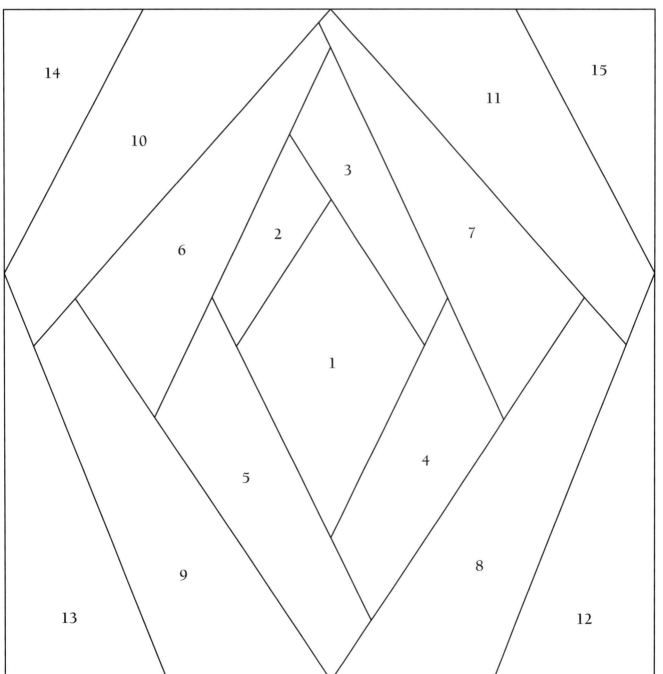

11

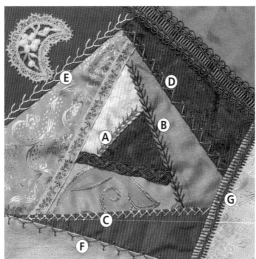

(A) Wheat Ear Stitch
(B) Fly Stitch
(C) Herringbone Stitch
(D) Chevron Stitch
(E) Feather Stitch
(F) Cretan Stitch
(G) Vandyke Stitch

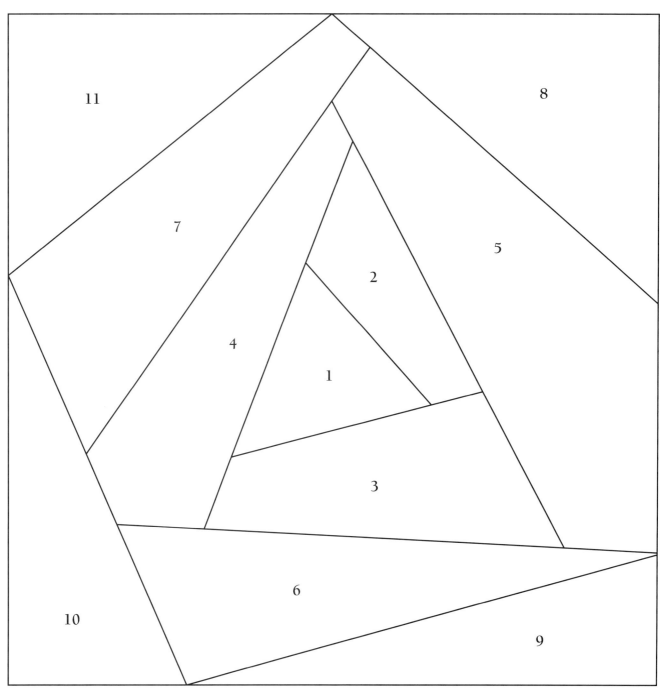

- (A) Blanket Stitch-closed
- (B) Fly Stitch
- (C) Feather Stitch
- (D) Cretan Stitch
- (E) Chevron Stitch
- (F) Wheat Ear Stitch
- (G) Herringbone Stitch
- (H) Blanket Stitch
- (I) Vandyke Stitch
- (J) Lazy Daisy

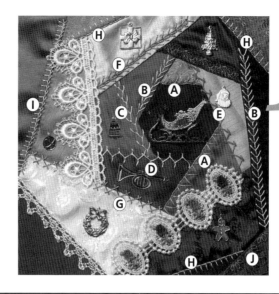

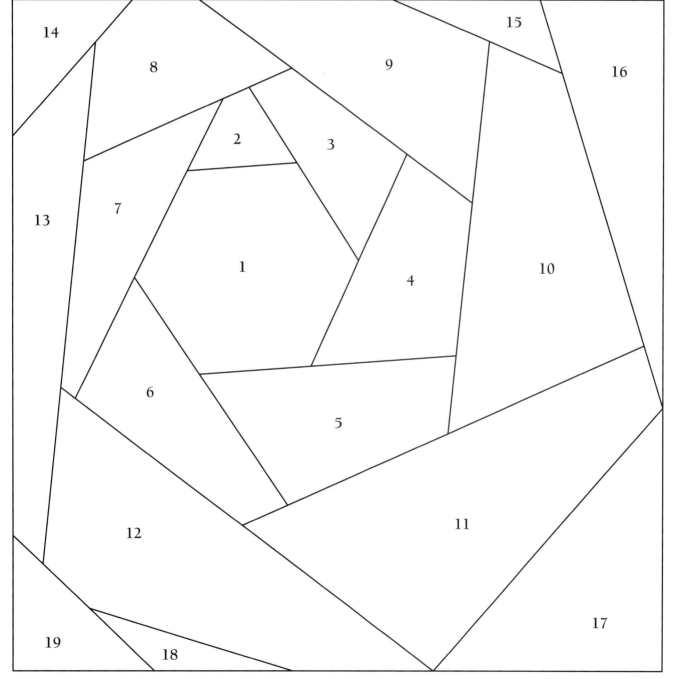

13

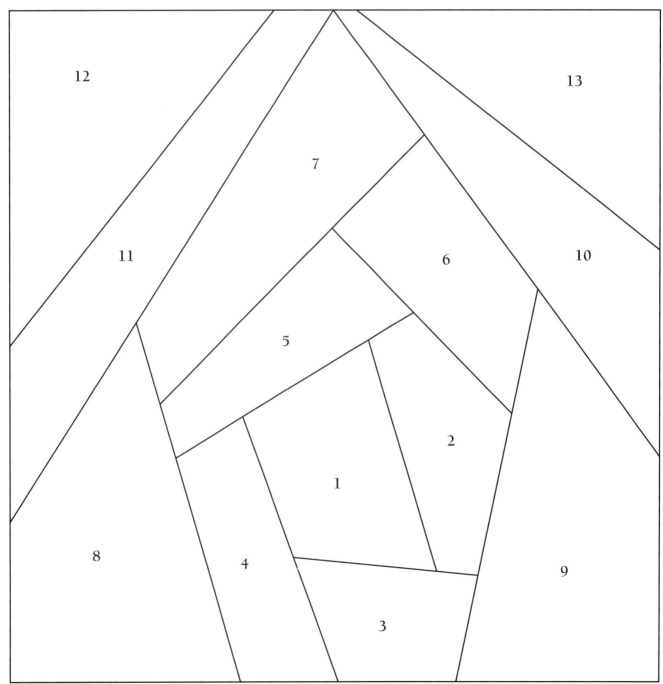

(A) Feather Stitch
(B) Herringbone Stitch
(C) Chevron Stitch
(D) Blanket Stitch
(E) Maidenhair Stitch
(F) Wheat Ear Stitch
(G) Stem Stitch
(H) Lazy Daisy
(I) Blanket Stitch-closed
(J) Colonial Knot
(K) Chain Stitch

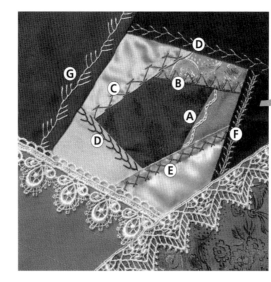

(A) Chain Stitch
(B) Blanket Stitch-closed
(C) Chevron Stitch
(D) Feather Stitch
(E) Herringbone Stitch
(F) Wheat Ear Stitch
(G) Maidenhair Stitch

14

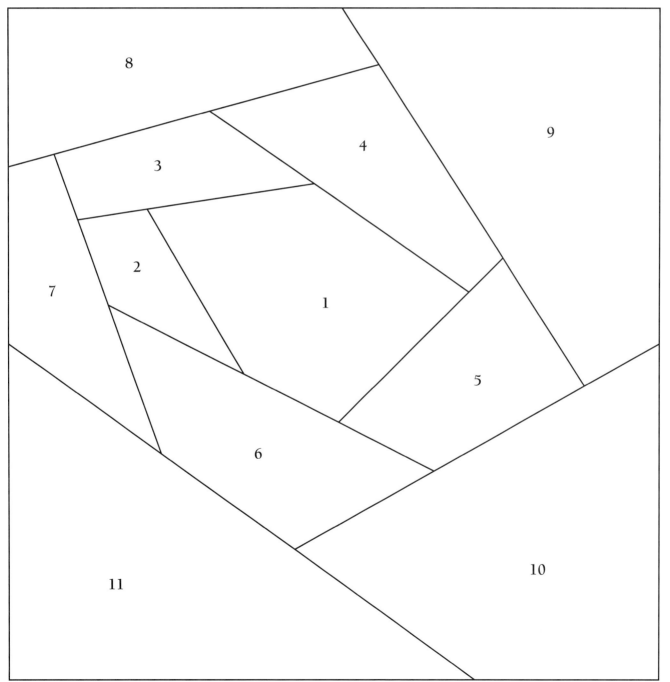

8

3

4

9

2

7

1

5

6

10

11

15

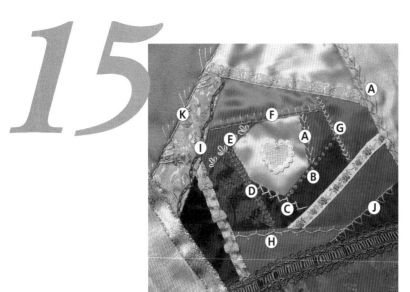

- (A) Feather Stitch
- (B) Colonial Knot
- (C) Herringbone Stitch
- (D) Wheat Ear Stitch
- (E) Lazy Daisy
- (F) Blanket Stitch
- (G) Cross Stitch
- (H) Cretan Stitch
- (I) Chain Stitch
- (J) Blanket Stitch-closed
- (K) Maidenhair Stitch

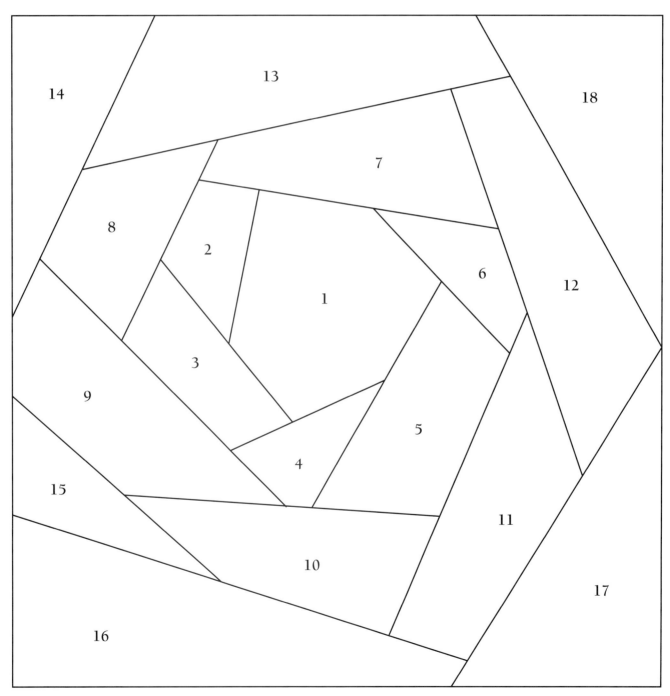

A) Blanket Stitch
B) Feather Stitch
C) Blanket Stitch-closed
D) Colonial Knot (silk ribbon)
E) Chain Stitch (two rows)
F) Chevron Stitch
G) Maidenhair Stitch
H) Fly Stitch

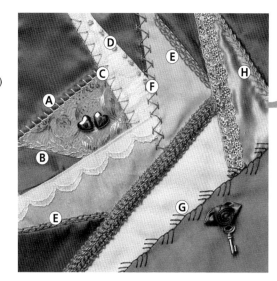

16

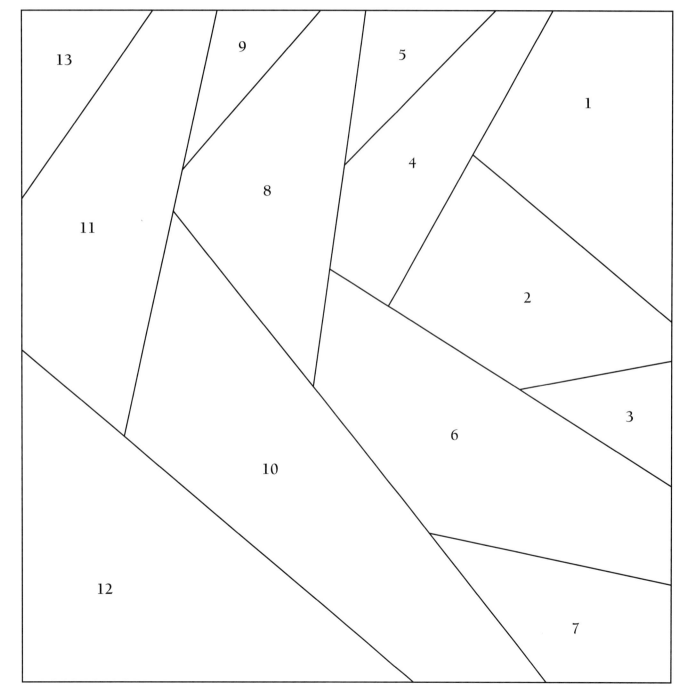

17

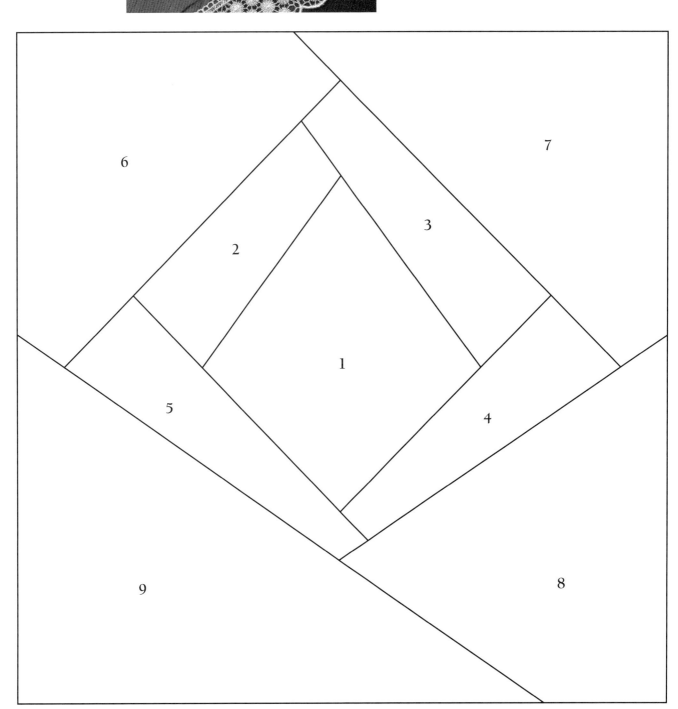

(A) Chevron Stitch
(B) Wheat Ear Stitch
(C) Vandyke Stitch
(D) Cretan Stitch

(A) Herringbone Stitch
(B) Feather Stitch
(C) Stem Stitch
(D) Lazy Daisy
(E) Wheat Ear Stitch
(F) Blanket Stitch
(G) Chevron Stitch
(H) Vandyke Stitch
(I) Maidenhair Stitch
(J) Blanket Stitch-closed
(K) Cretan Stitch
(L) Chain Stitch (two rows)

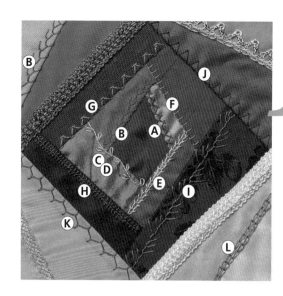

18

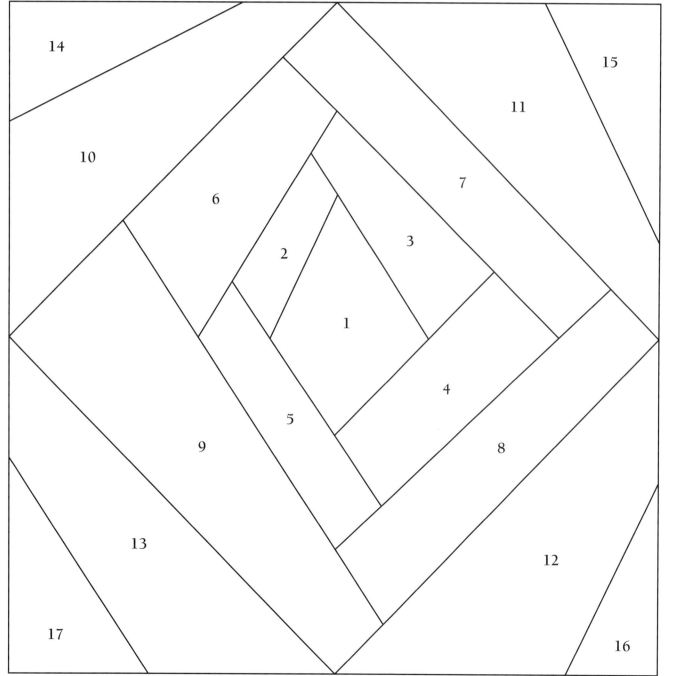

19

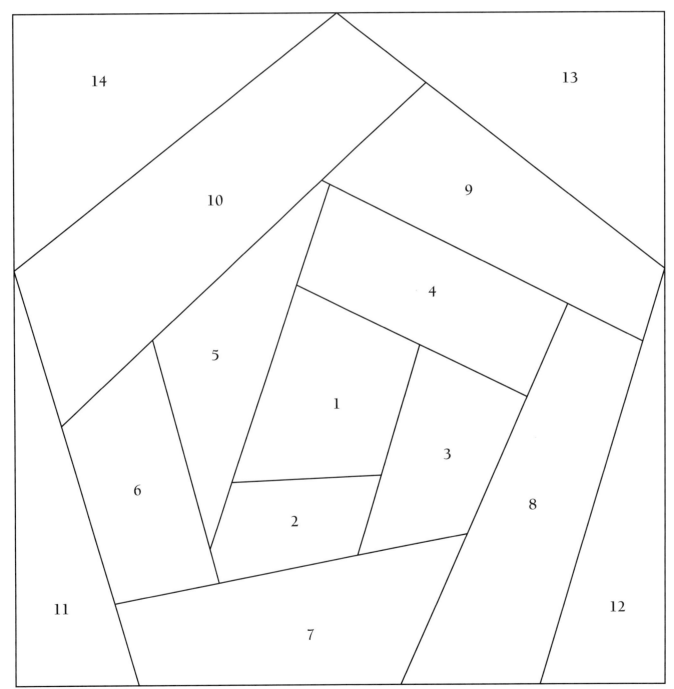

- (A) Blanket Stitch
- (B) Feather Stitch
- (C) Chevron Stitch
- (D) Vandyke Stitch
- (E) Fly Stitch
- (F) Blanket Stitch-closed
- (G) Wheat Ear Stitch
- (H) Cross Stitch
- (I) Lazy Daisy
- (J) Herringbone Stitch
- (K) Stem Stitch

(A) Blanket Stitch
(B) Herringbone Stitch
(C) Vandyke Stitch
(D) Feather Stitch
(E) Cretan Stitch
(F) Fly Stitch
(G) Maidenhair Stitch
(H) Chain Stitch
(I) Lazy Daisy Stitch
(J) Chevron Stitch

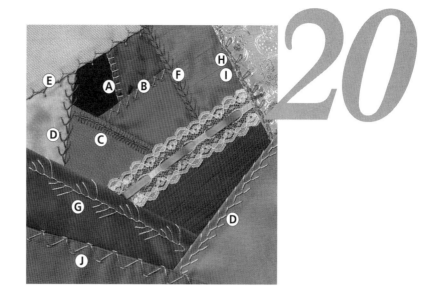

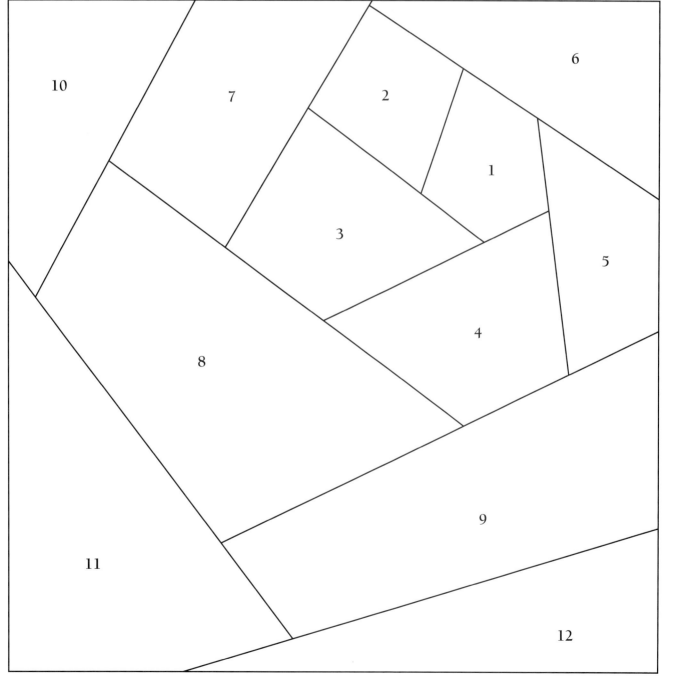

21

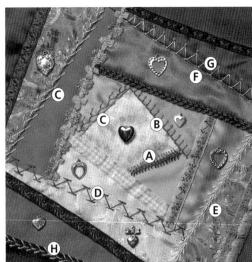

- **A** Vandyke Stitch
- **B** Blanket Stitch
- **C** Feather Stitch
- **D** Chevron Stitch
- **E** Wheat Ear Stitch
- **F** Blanket Stitch-closed
- **G** French Knot
- **H** Fly Stitch

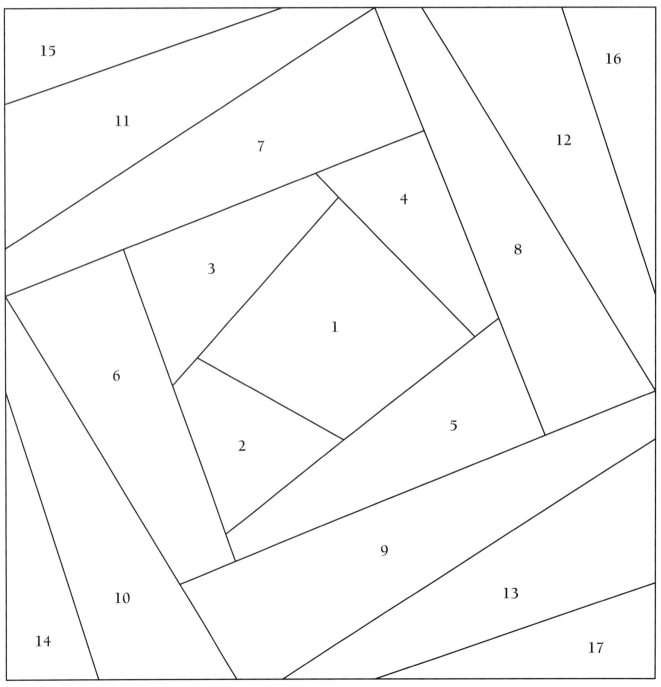

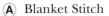

- (A) Blanket Stitch
- (B) Wheat Ear Stitch
- (C) Vandyke Stitch
- (D) Maidenhair Stitch
- (E) Feather Stitch
- (F) Chevron Stitch
- (G) Herringbone Stitch
- (H) Straight Stitch
- (I) Lazy Daisy (with beads)
- (J) Colonial Knot
- (K) Cretan Stitch
- (L) Blanket Stitch-closed
- (M) Lazy Daisy

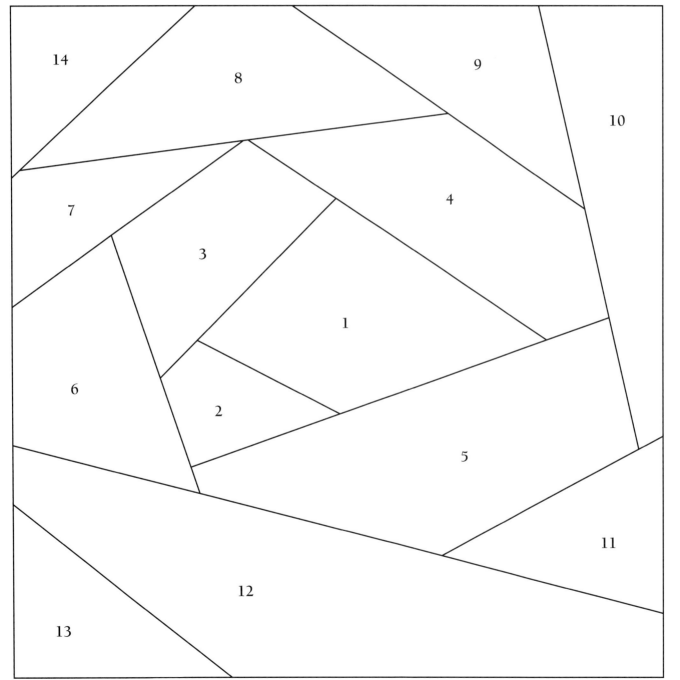

23

- (A) Blanket Stitch
- (B) Blanket Stitch-closed
- (C) Feather Stitch
- (D) Fly Stitch
- (E) Maidenhair Stitch
- (F) Herringbone Stitch

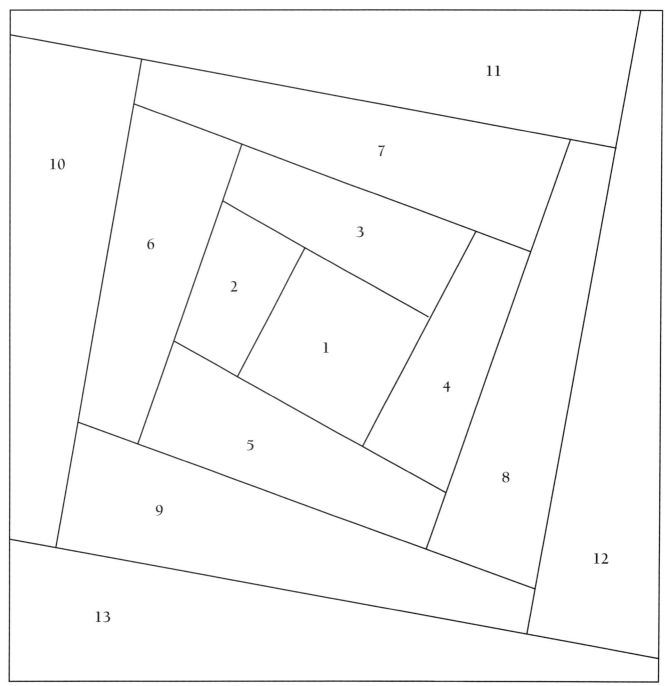

(A) Straight Stitch (silk ribbon)
(B) Colonial Knot (silk ribbon)
(C) Maidenhair Stitch
(D) Fly Stitch
(E) Chevron Stitch
(F) Feather Stitch (with beads)
(G) Lazy Daisy
(H) Colonial Knot
(I) Wheat Ear
(J) Herringbone Stitch
(K) French Knot
(L) Running Stitch (with beads)

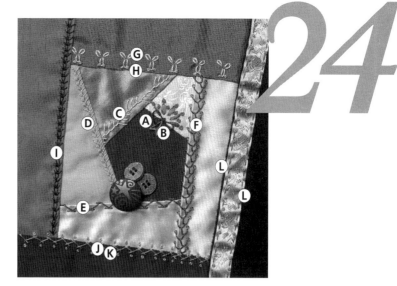

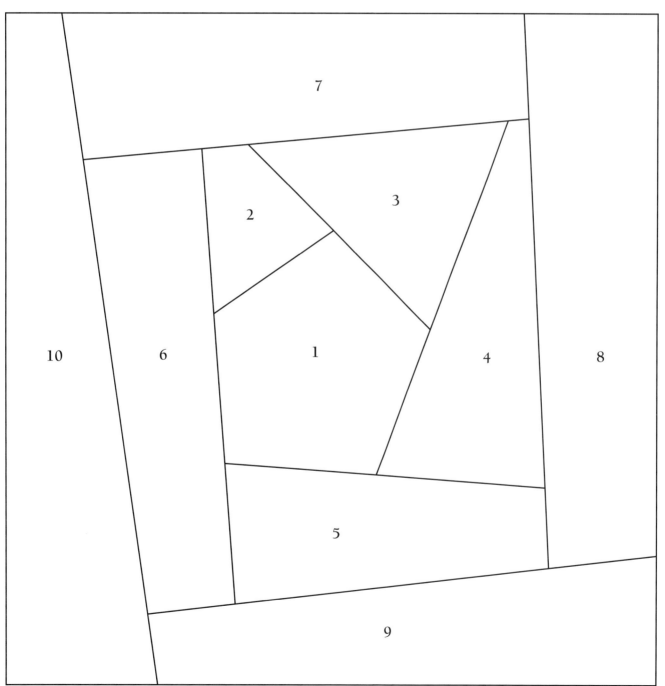

A Blanket Stitch
B Chain Stitch (two rows)
C Herringbone Stitch
D Maidenhair Stitch
E Blanket Stitch-closed
F Straight Stitch
G Feather Stitch (with beads)

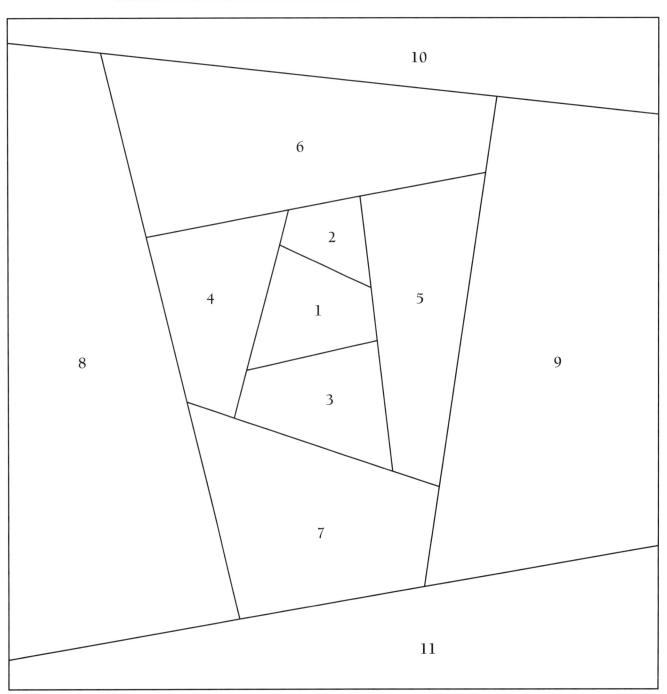

(A) Herringbone Stitch
(B) Blanket Stitch-closed
(C) Chevron Stitch
(D) Wheat Ear Stitch
(E) Fly Stitch
(F) Feather Stitch
(G) Vandyke Stitch
(H) Colonial Knot
(I) Chain Stitch (two rows)
(J) Silk ribbon tacked with seed beads

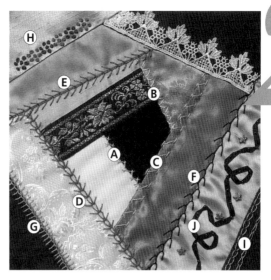

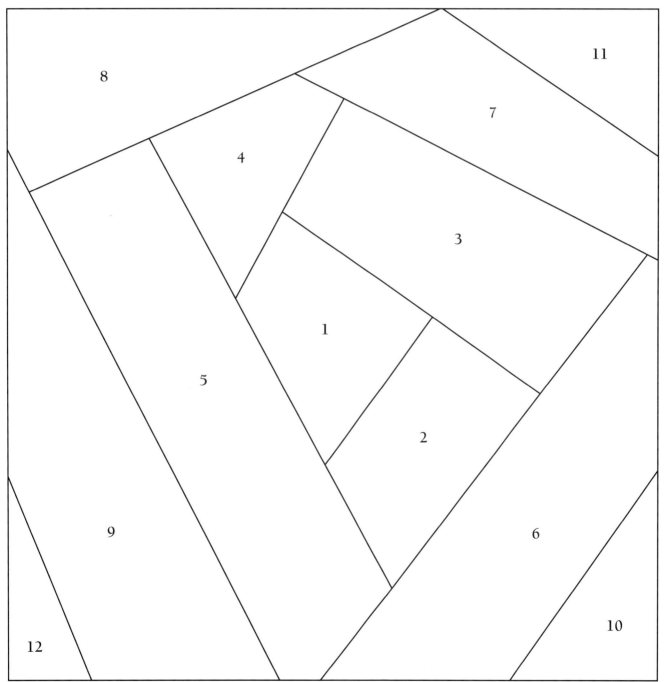

27

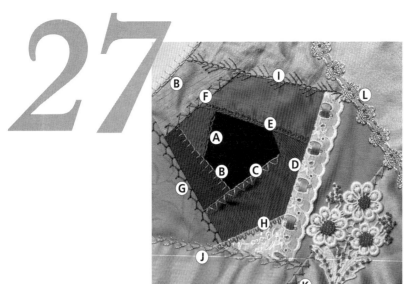

- Ⓐ Chain Stitch (two rows)
- Ⓑ Blanket Stitch
- Ⓒ Blanket Stitch-closed
- Ⓓ Fly Stitch
- Ⓔ Wheat Ear Stitch
- Ⓕ Chevron Stitch
- Ⓖ Cretan Stitch
- Ⓗ Lazy Daisy
- Ⓘ Maidenhair Stitch
- Ⓙ Feather Stitch
- Ⓚ Herringbone Stitch
- Ⓛ French Knot

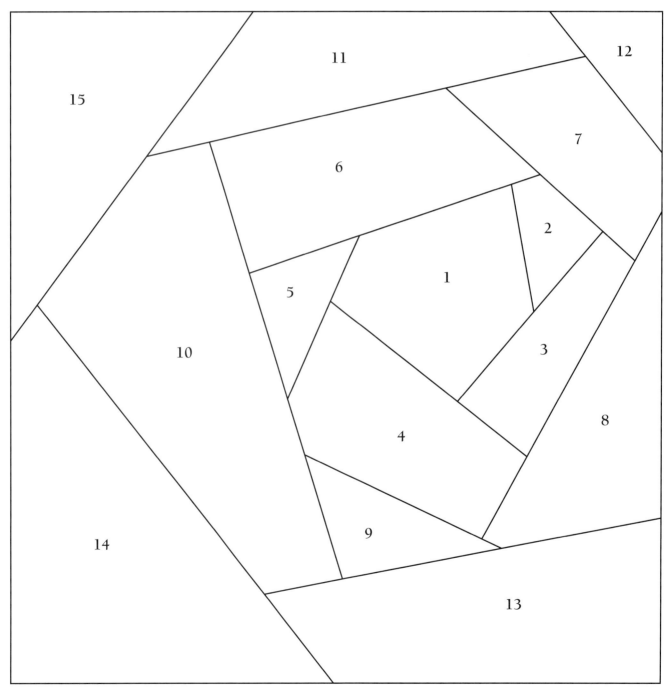

(A) Blanket Stitch
(B) Blanket Stitch-closed
(C) Herringbone Stitch
(D) Maidenhair Stitch
(E) Chevron Stitch
(F) Cretan Stitch
(G) Feather Stitch

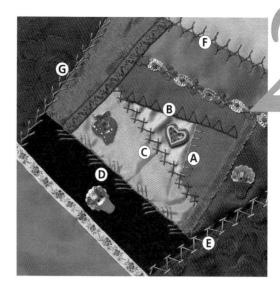

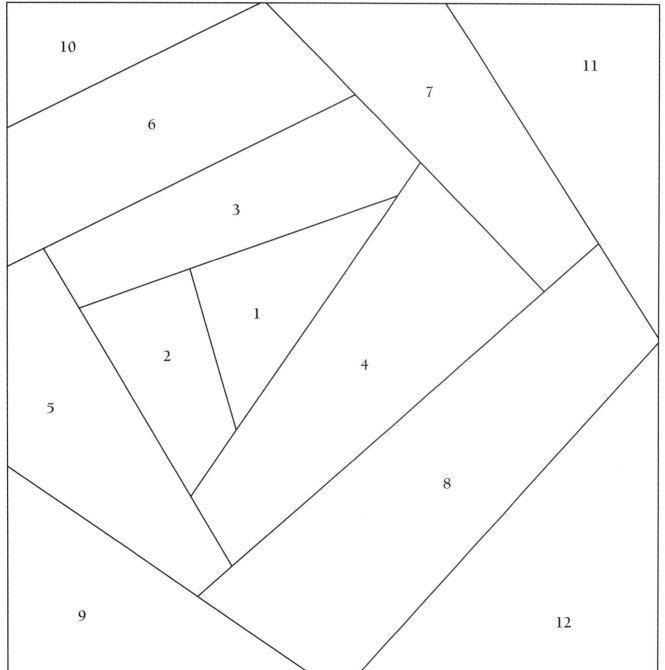

- (A) Lazy Daisy
- (B) French Knot
- (C) Feather Stitch
- (D) Fly Stitch
- (E) Cretan Stitch
- (F) Blanket Stitch (with beads)
- (G) Herringbone Stitch (with beads)
- (H) Maidenhair Stitch (with beads)

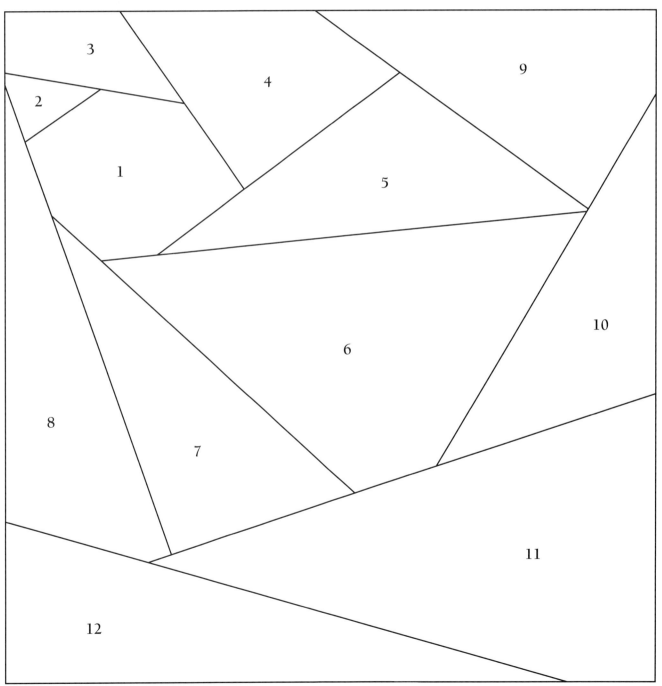

(A) Lazy Daisy
(B) Chevron Stitch
(C) Wheat Ear Stitch
(D) Herringbone Stitch
(E) Feather Stitch
(F) Blanket Stitch-closed
(G) Colonial Knot
(H) Maidenhair Stitch

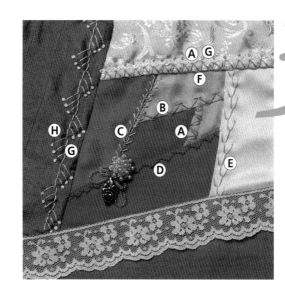

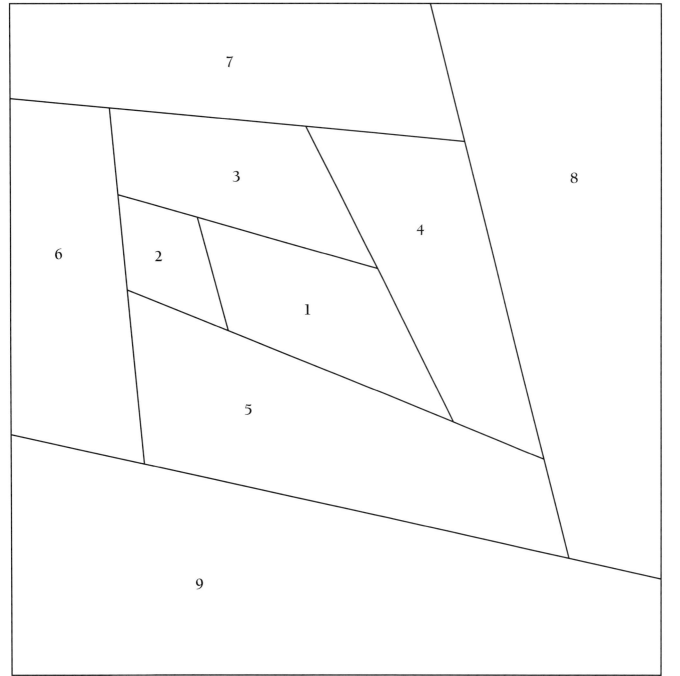

31

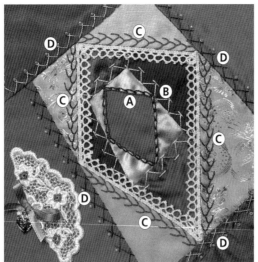

(A) Chain Stitch
(B) Chevron Stitch
(C) Feather Stitch
(D) Herringbone Stitch (with beads)

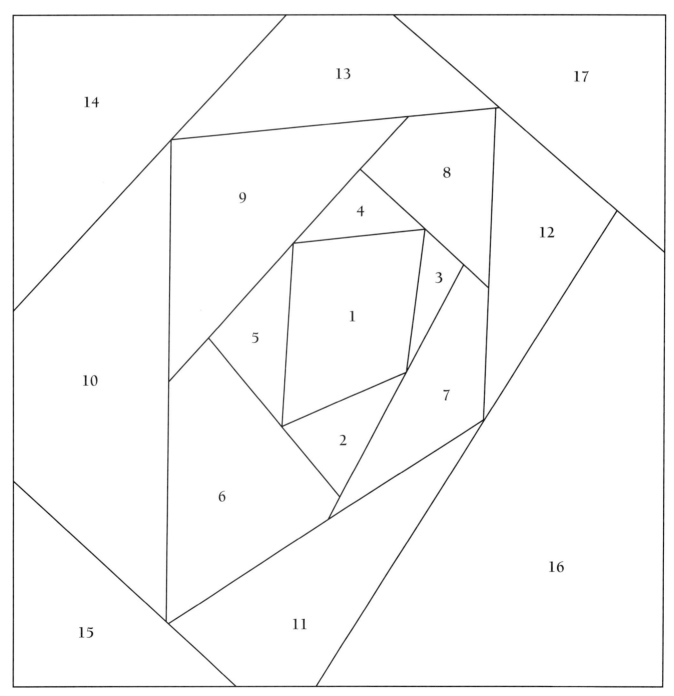

- Ⓐ Feather Stitch
- Ⓑ Herringbone Stitch
- Ⓒ Vandyke Stitch
- Ⓓ Blanket Stitch
- Ⓔ Fly Stitch
- Ⓕ Cretan Stitch
- Ⓖ Stem Stitch
- Ⓗ Lazy Daisy
- Ⓘ Colonial Knot

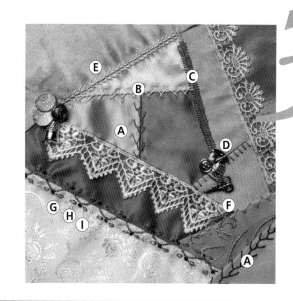

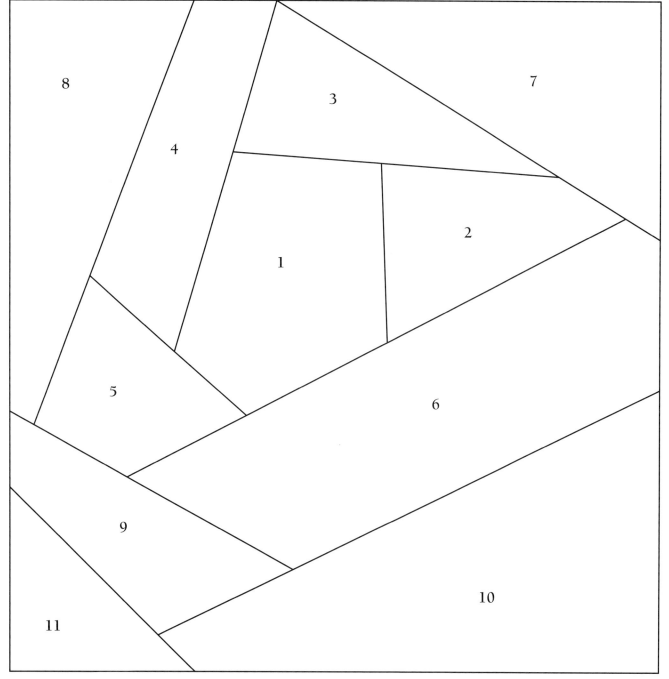

33

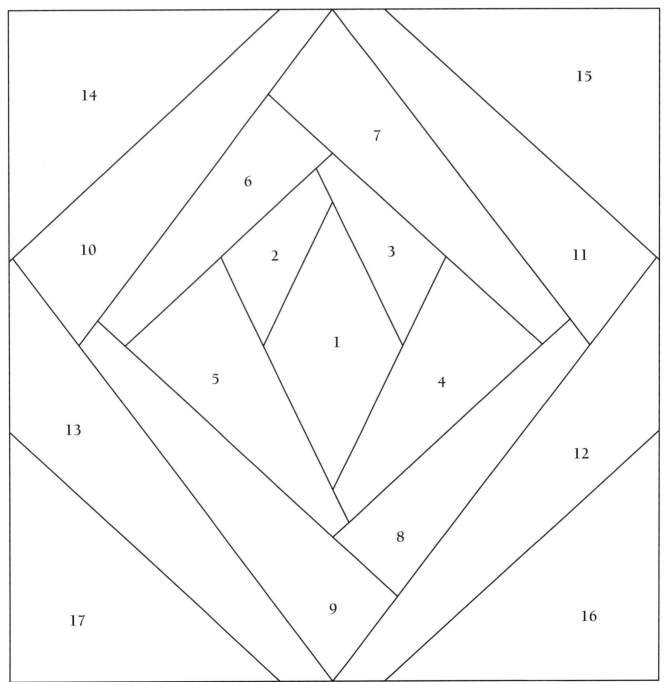

- (A) Blanket Stitch
- (B) Chain Stitch
- (C) Fly Stitch
- (D) Blanket Stitch-closed
- (E) Feather Stitch
- (F) Cretan Stitch
- (G) Chevron Stitch
- (H) Maidenhair Stitch
- (I) Lazy Daisy
- (J) Straight Stitch
- (K) Colonial Knot

(A) Lazy Daisy
(B) Colonial Knot (silk ribbon)
(C) Chevron Stitch
(D) Feather Stitch
(E) Blanket Stitch
(F) Cretan Stitch
(G) Maidenhair Stitch (with beads)
(H) Running Stitch
(I) Blanket Stitch-closed
(J) Wheat Ear Stitch
(K) Straight Stitch
(L) Colonial Knot (6 strands floss)

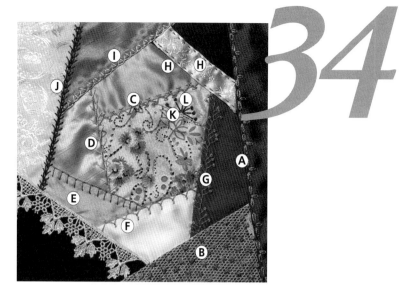

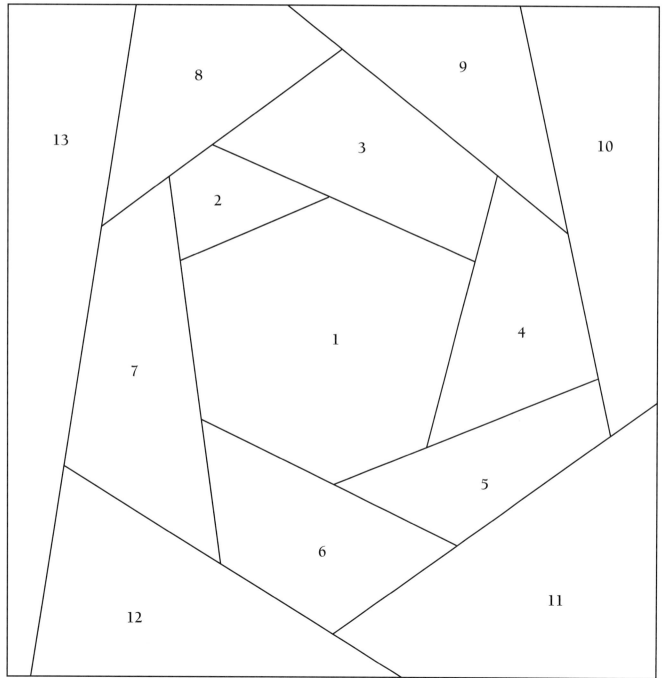

35

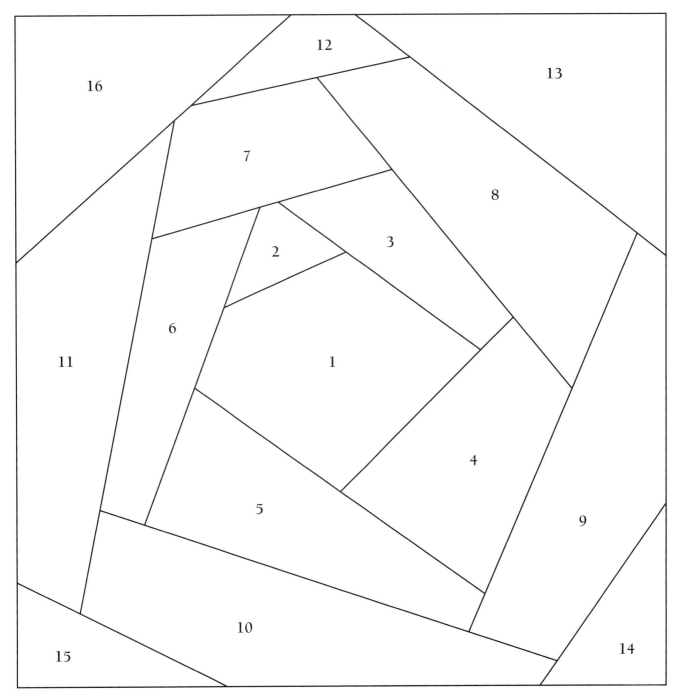

(A) Blanket Stitch
(B) Maidenhair Stitch
(C) Cretan Stitch
(D) Vandyke Stitch
(E) Blanket Stitch-closed

A Blanket Stitch
B Lazy Daisy
C French Knot
D Feather Stitch
E Vandyke Stitch
F Fly Stitch
G Cretan Stitch
H Chevron Stitch

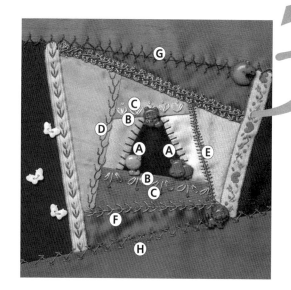

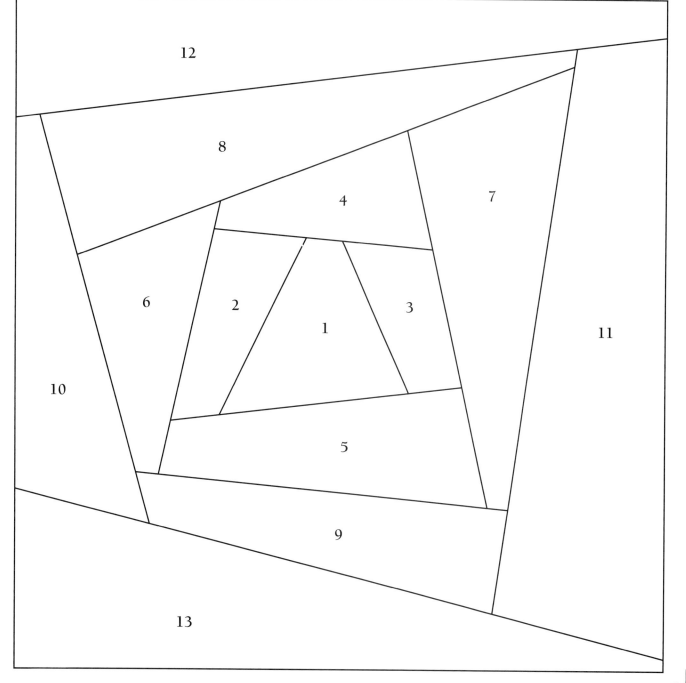

37

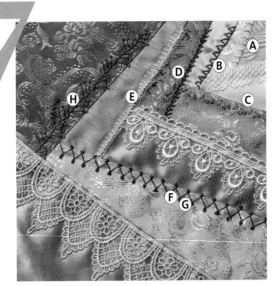

- (A) Blanket Stitch
- (B) Blanket Stitch-closed
- (C) Lazy Daisy
- (D) Wheat Ear Stitch
- (E) Vandyke Stitch
- (F) Herringbone Stitch
- (G) Colonial Knot
- (H) Maidenhair Stitch (with beads)

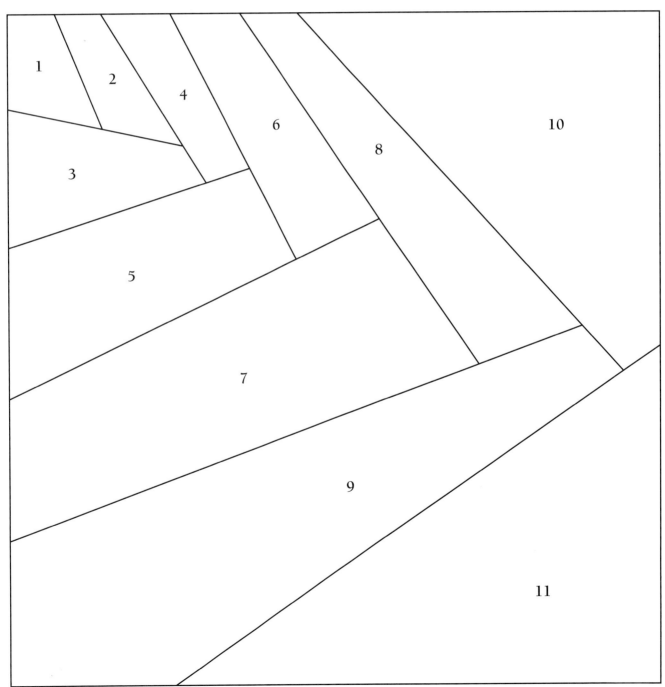

Crazy Quilt Blocks 17 - 36

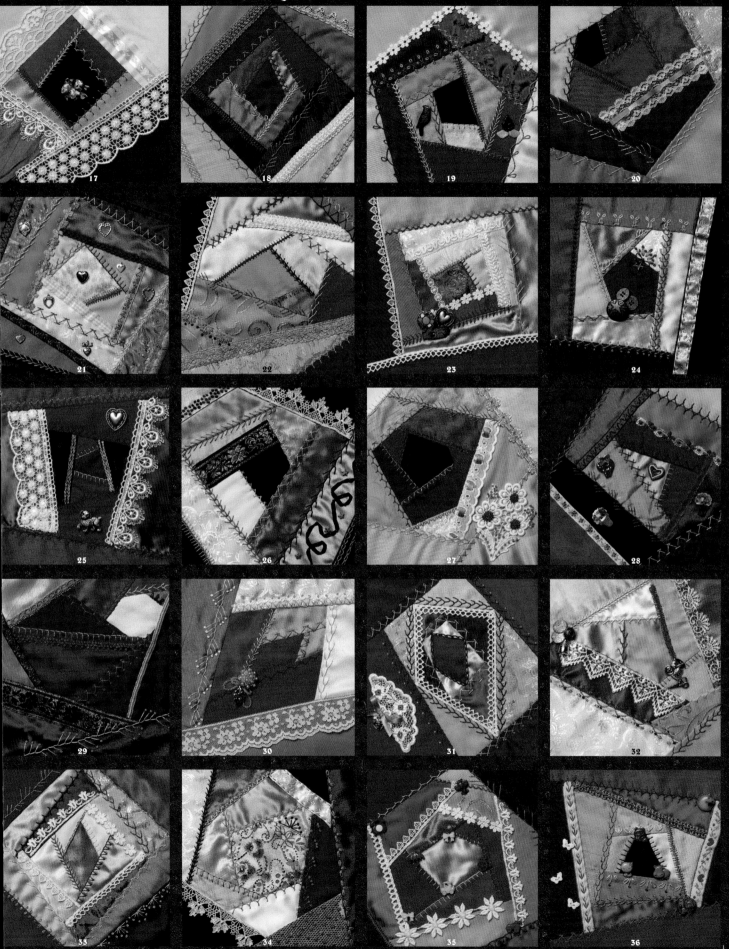

Crazy Quilt Blocks 37-51

37
38
39
40
41
42
43
44
45
46
47
48
49
50
51

Crazy Quilt Blocks 52 - 66

(A) Fly Stitch
(B) Herringbone Stitch
(C) Feather Stitch
(D) Stem Stitch
(E) Lazy Daisy
(F) Vandyke Stitch
(G) Wheat Ear Stitch

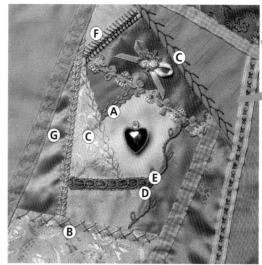

38

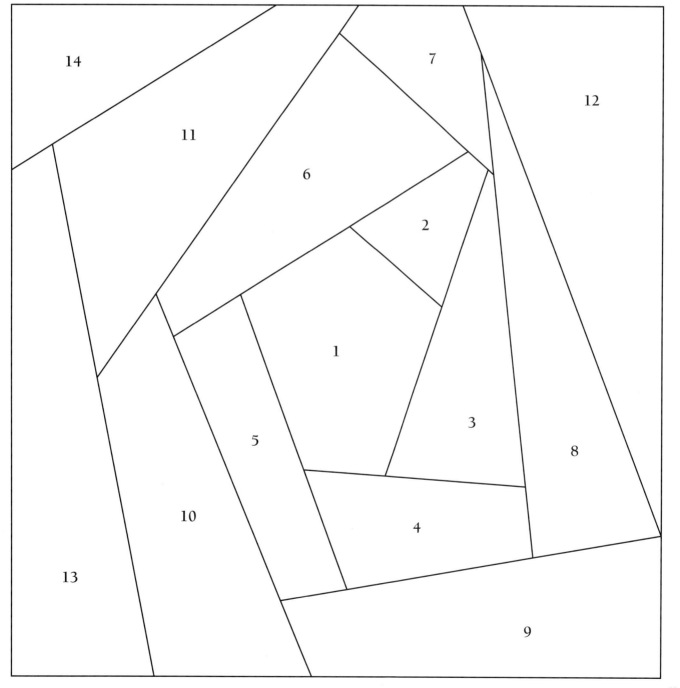

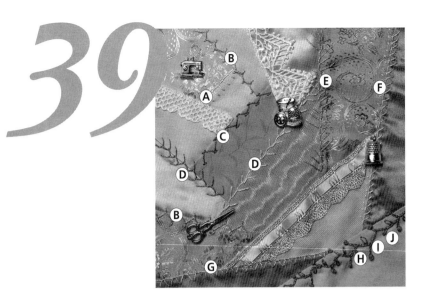

- (A) Blanket Stitch
- (B) Cretan Stitch
- (C) Chevron Stitch
- (D) Feather Stitch
- (E) Maidenhair Stitch
- (F) Fly Stitch
- (G) Blanket Stitch-closed
- (H) Stem Stitch
- (I) Lazy Daisy
- (J) Colonial Knot (silk ribbon)

39

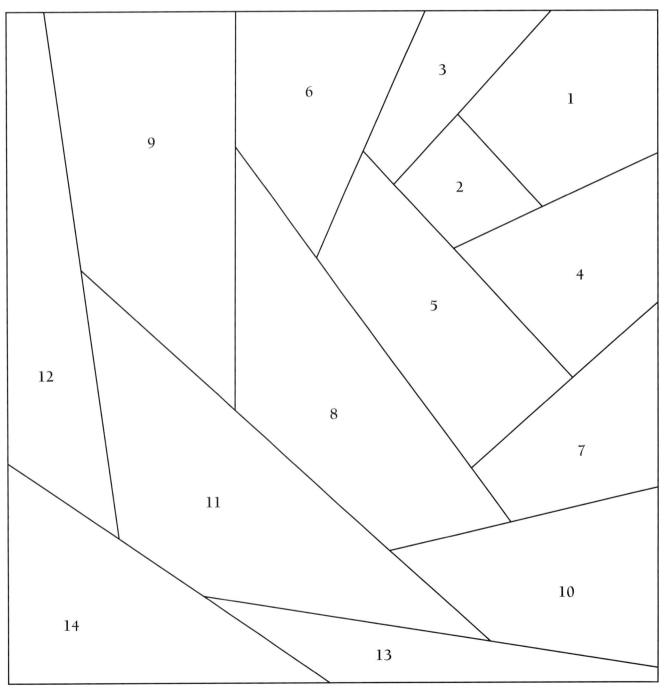

(A) Chain Stitch
(B) Blanket Stitch
(C) Wheat Ear Stitch
(D) Chevron Stitch
(E) Vandyke Stitch
(F) Feather Stitch
(G) Herringbone Stitch
(H) Maidenhair Stitch
(I) Blanket Stitch-closed
(J) Cretan Stitch
(K) Colonial Knot (to attach buttons)

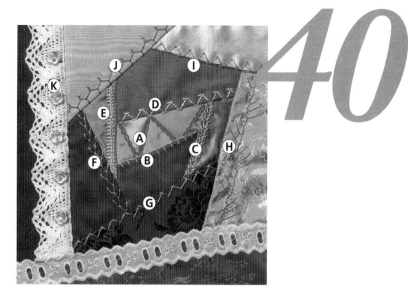

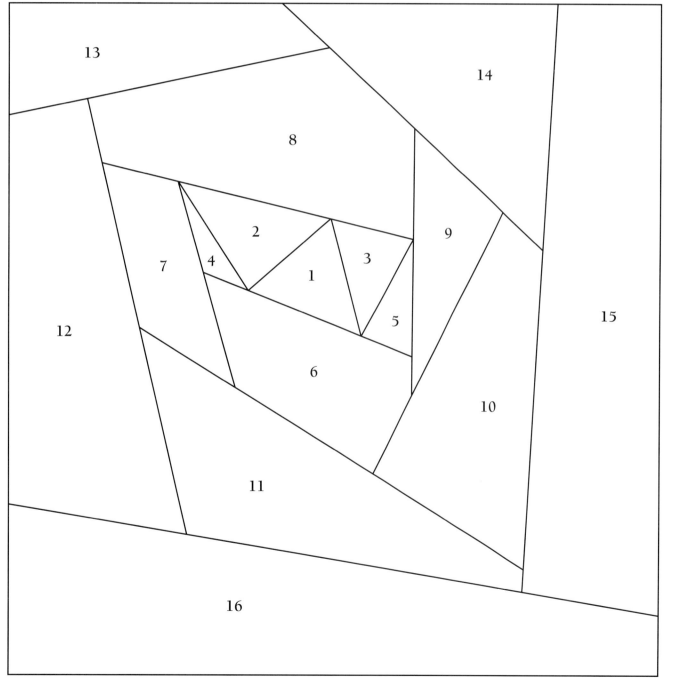

41

A) Feather Stitch
B) Blanket Stitch-closed
C) Fly Stitch
D) Cretan Stitch
E) Herringbone Stitch
F) Wheat Ear Stitch
G) Blanket Stitch
H) Lazy Daisy
I) Chevron Stitch

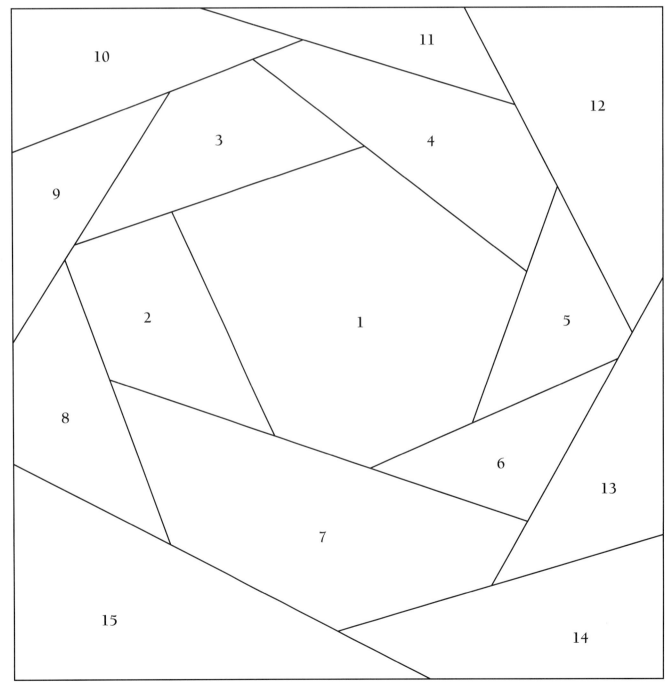

(A) Feather Stitch
(B) Herringbone Stitch (with beads)
(C) Cretan Stitch (with beads)
(D) Chevron Stitch
(E) Blanket Stitch (with beads)

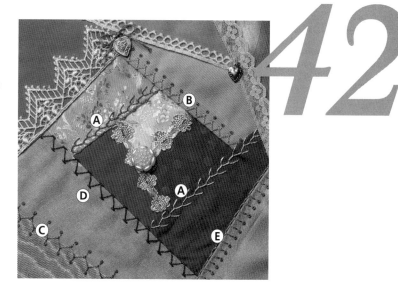

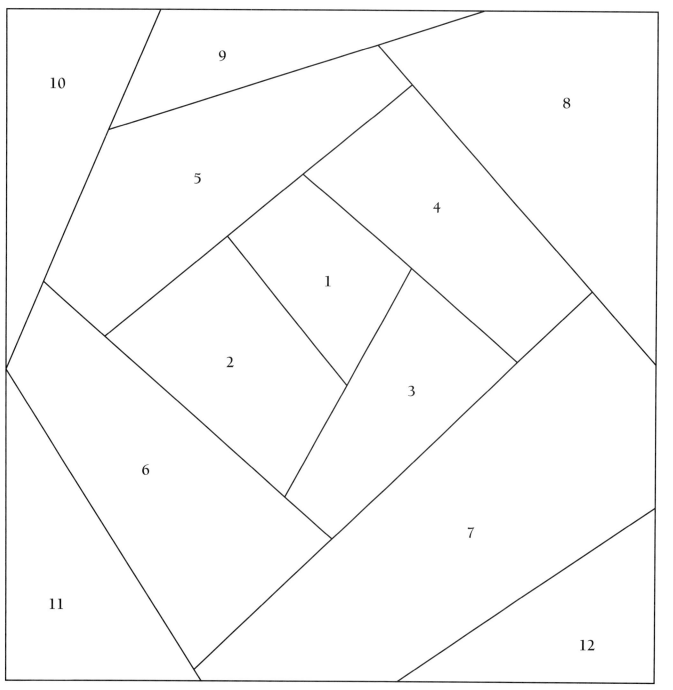

43

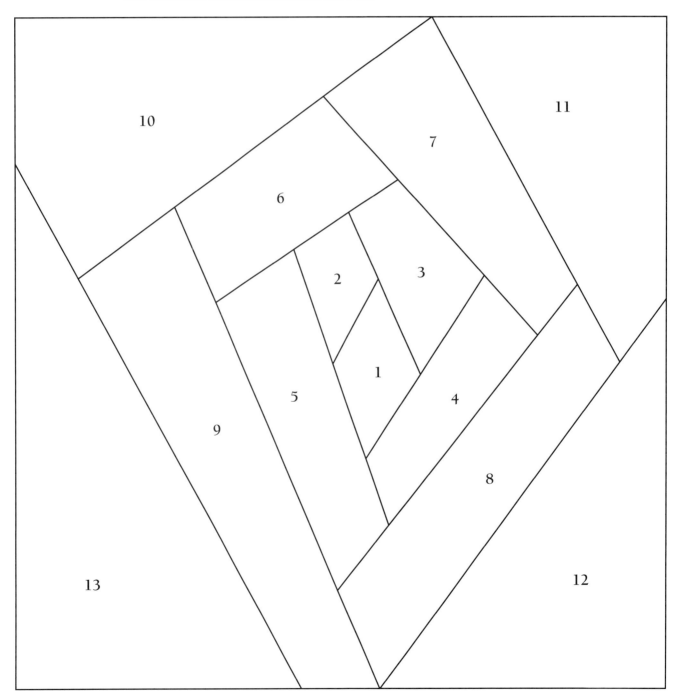

- (A) Straight Stitch
- (B) Colonial Knot
- (C) Lazy Daisy
- (D) Chevron Stitch
- (E) Herringbone Stitch
- (F) Chain Stitch
- (G) Blanket Stitch
- (H) Feather Stitch
- (I) Wheat Ear Stitch
- (J) Fly Stitch
- (K) Maidenhair Stitch

Ⓐ Blanket Stitch
Ⓑ Feather Stitch
Ⓒ Chevron Stitch
Ⓓ Stem Stitch
Ⓔ Colonial Knot
Ⓕ Herringbone Stitch

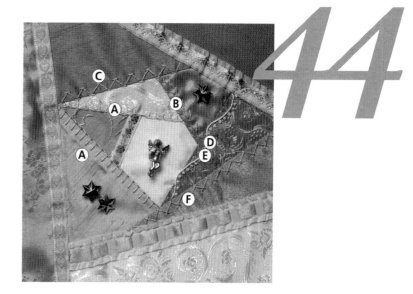

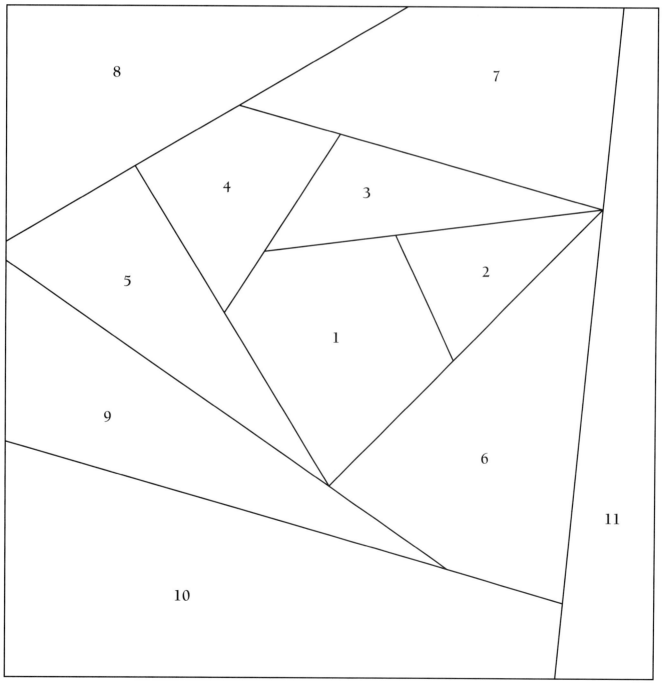

45

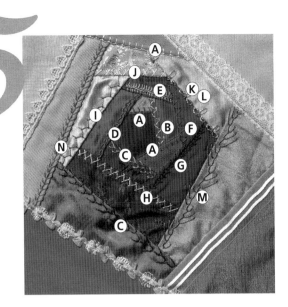

- (A) Blanket Stitch
- (B) Chevron Stitch
- (C) Feather Stitch
- (D) Chain Stitch
- (E) Vandyke Stitch
- (F) Blanket Stitch-closed
- (G) Wheat Ear Stitch
- (H) Herringbone Stitch
- (I) Cretan Stitch
- (J) Cross Stitch
- (K) Lazy Daisy
- (L) Colonial Knot
- (M) Maidenhair Stitch
- (N) Fly Stitch

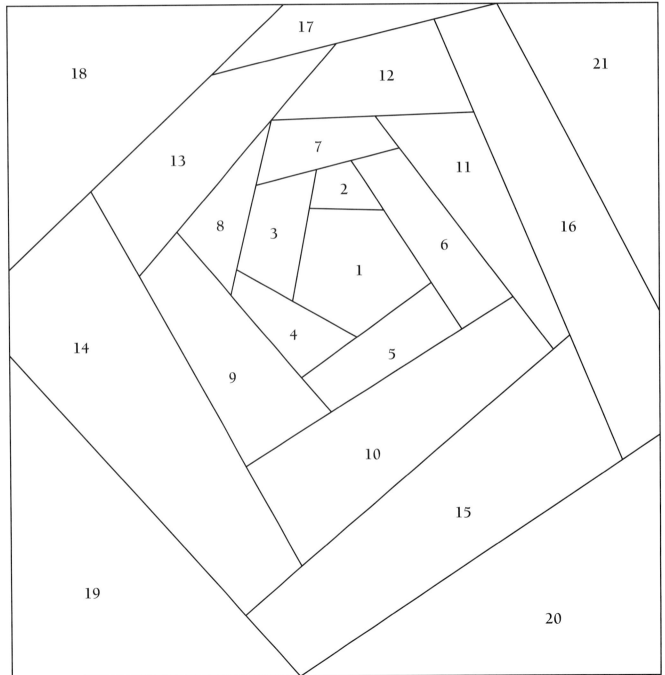

- (A) Feather Stitch
- (B) Blanket Stitch-closed
- (C) Maidenhair Stitch (with beads)
- (D) Cretan Stitch
- (E) Lazy Daisy

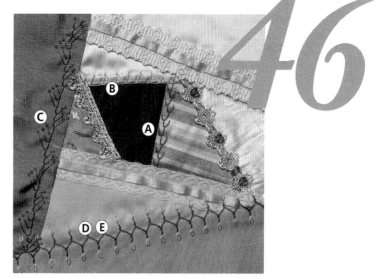

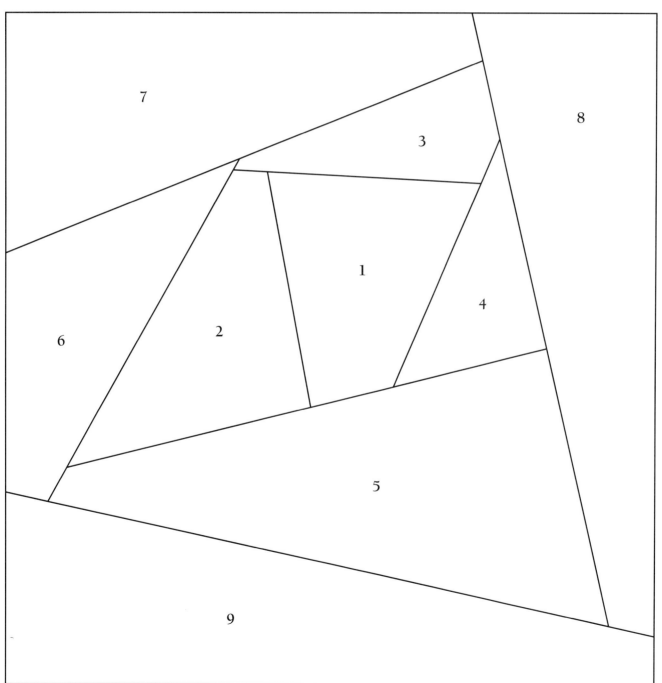

47

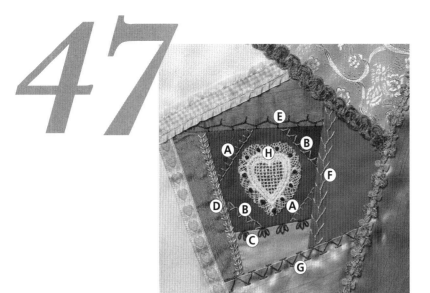

(A) Blanket Stitch
(B) Blanket Stitch-closed
(C) Lazy Daisy
(D) Wheat Ear Stitch
(E) Cretan Stitch
(F) Feather Stitch
(G) Chevron Stitch
(H) Colonial Knot

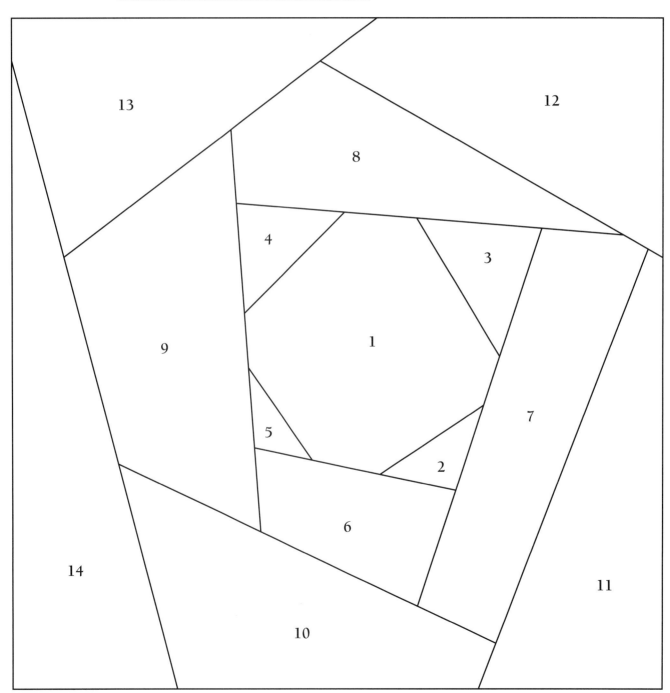

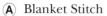

(A) Blanket Stitch
(B) Fly Stitch
(C) Herringbone Stitch
(D) Chevron Stitch
(E) Feather Stitch
(F) Maidenhair Stitch
(G) Chain Stitch (two rows)
(H) Straight Stitch (with beads)
(I) Ribbon attached with beads

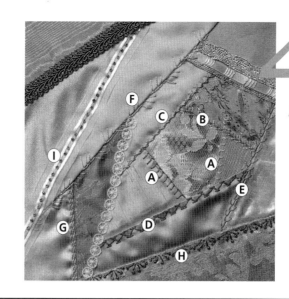

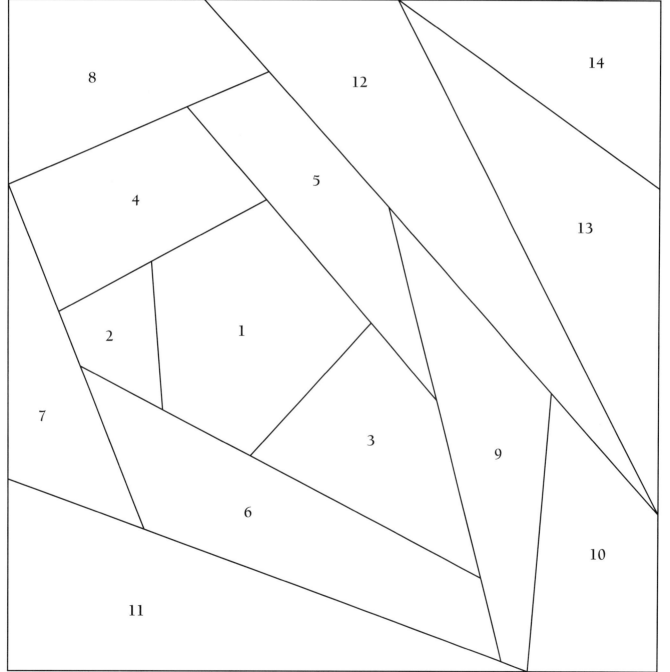

49

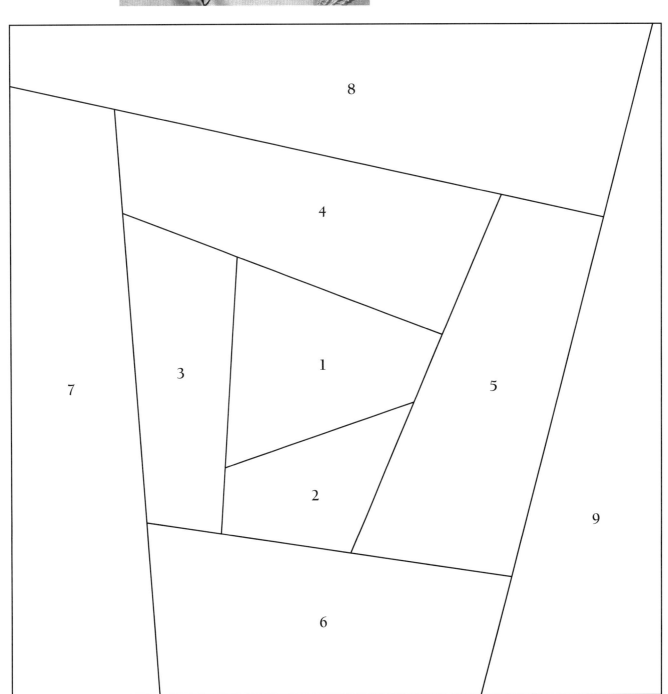

(A) Feather Stitch
(B) Chevron Stitch
(C) Cretan Stitch
(D) Maidenhair Stitch (with beads)

A Lazy Daisy
B Vandyke Stitch
C Blanket Stitch
D Feather Stitch
E Cretan Stitch
F Wheat Ear Stitch
G Chevron Stitch
H Chain Stitch
I Cross Stitch
J Blanket Stitch-closed
K Herringbone Stitch

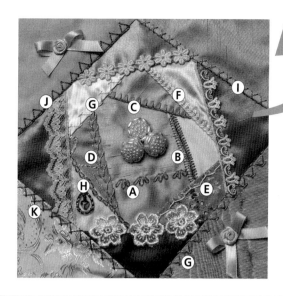

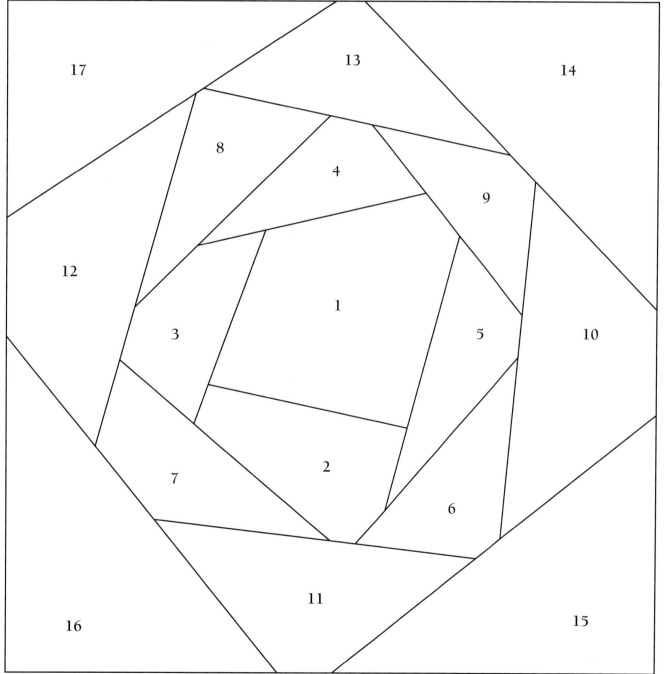

51

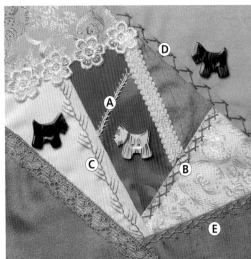

(A) Wheat Ear Stitch
(B) Herringbone Stitch
(C) Maidenhair Stitch
(D) Chevron Stitch
(E) Feather Stitch

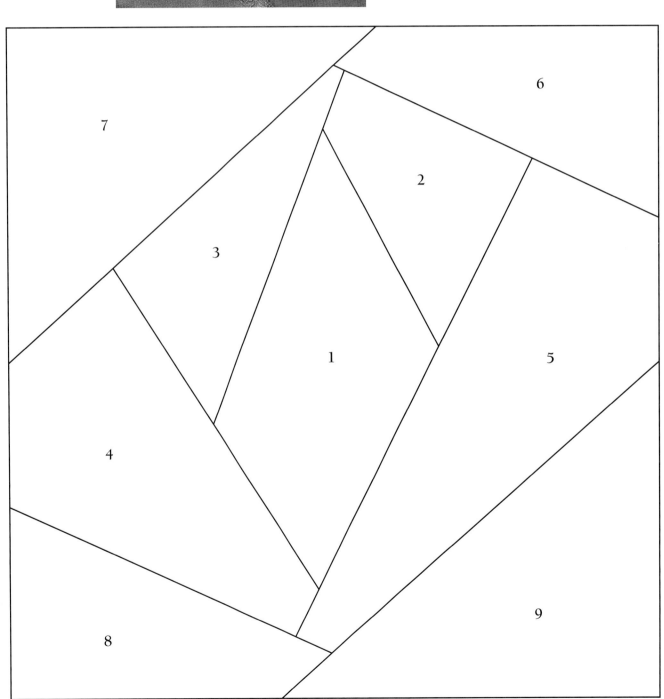

(A) Chain Stitch (two rows)

(B) Blanket Stitch

(C) Cross Stitch

(D) Colonial Knot

(E) Feather Stitch

(F) Cretan Stitch

(G) Lazy Daisy

(H) Blanket Stitch-closed
(with beads)

(I) Chevron Stitch

(J) Cross Stitch (with beads)

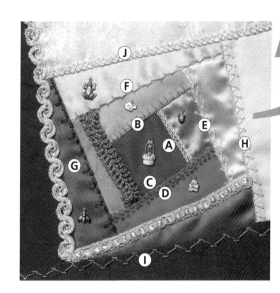

52

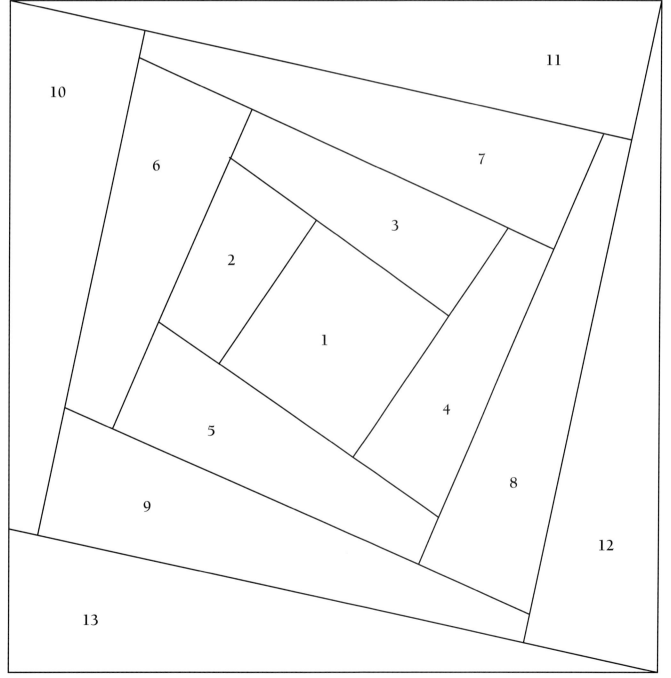

53

- Ⓐ Feather Stitch
- Ⓑ Blanket Stitch-closed
- Ⓒ Colonial Knot (silk ribbon)
- Ⓓ Chain Stitch (two rows)
- Ⓔ Fly Stitch
- Ⓕ Wheat Ear Stitch
- Ⓖ Cretan Stitch
- Ⓗ Vandyke Stitch

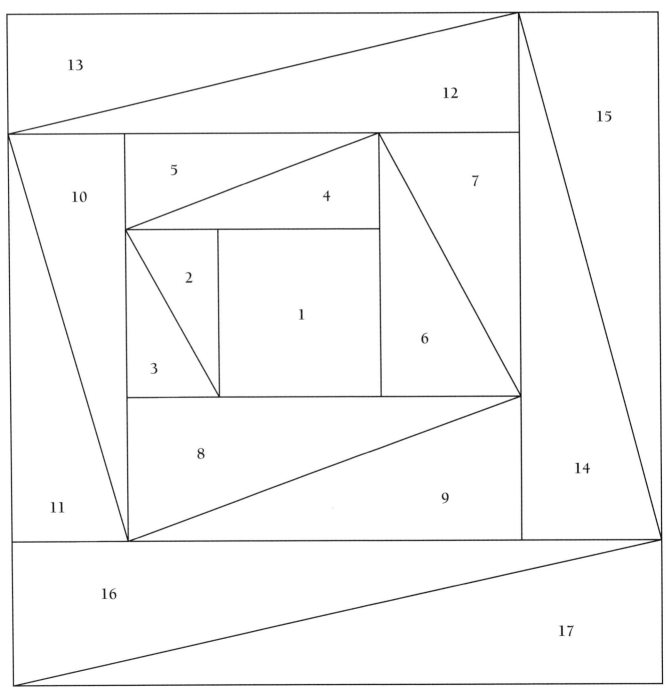

(A) Fly Stitch
(B) Lazy Daisy
(C) Colonial Knot (silk ribbon)
(D) Blanket Stitch-closed
(E) Feather Stitch
(F) Cretan Stitch
(G) Chevron Stitch
(H) Cross Stitch

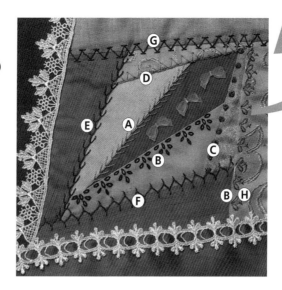

54

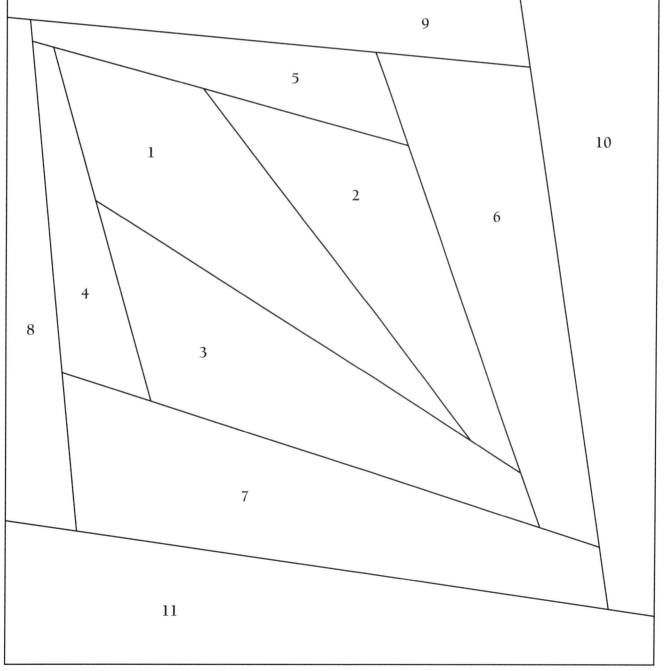

55

- (A) Blanket Stitch
- (B) Blanket Stitch-closed
- (C) Wheat Ear Stitch
- (D) Fly Stitch
- (E) Feather Stitch
- (F) Chevron Stitch
- (G) Herringbone Stitch
- (H) Vandyke Stitch

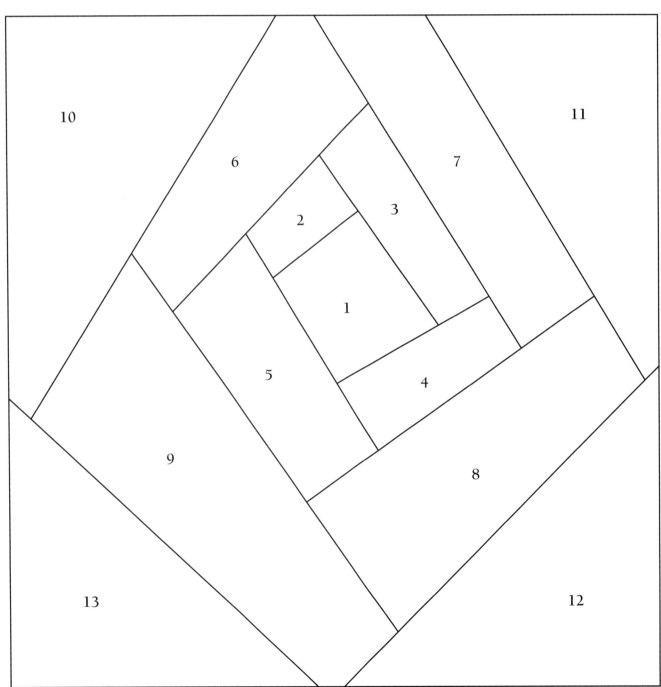

(A) Blanket Stitch-closed
(B) Herringbone Stitch
(C) Blanket Stitch
(D) Feather Stitch
(E) Chevron Stitch
(F) Wheat Ear Stitch
(G) Cretan Stitch
(H) Fly Stitch

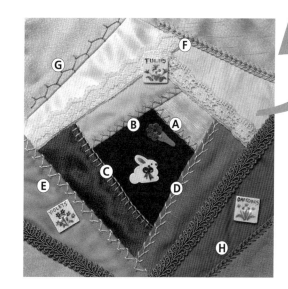

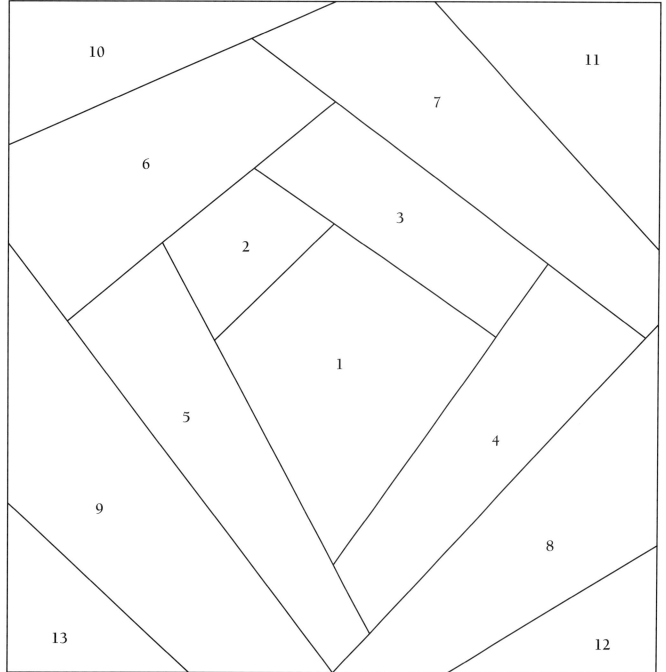

(A) Blanket Stitch
(B) Feather Stitch
(C) Maidenhair Stitch
(D) Herringbone Stitch
(E) Chevron Stitch
(F) Fly Stitch
(G) Cretan Stitch
(H) Straight Stitch (to attach ribbon)
(I) French Knot (to attach ribbon)

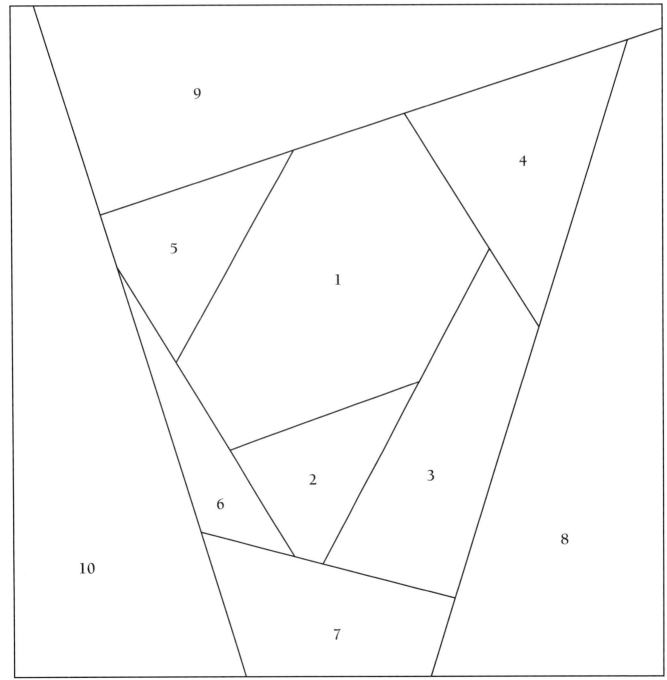

(A) Blanket Stitch
(B) Chevron Stitch
(C) Vandyke Stitch
(D) Feather Stitch
(E) Wheat Ear Stitch
(F) Fly Stitch

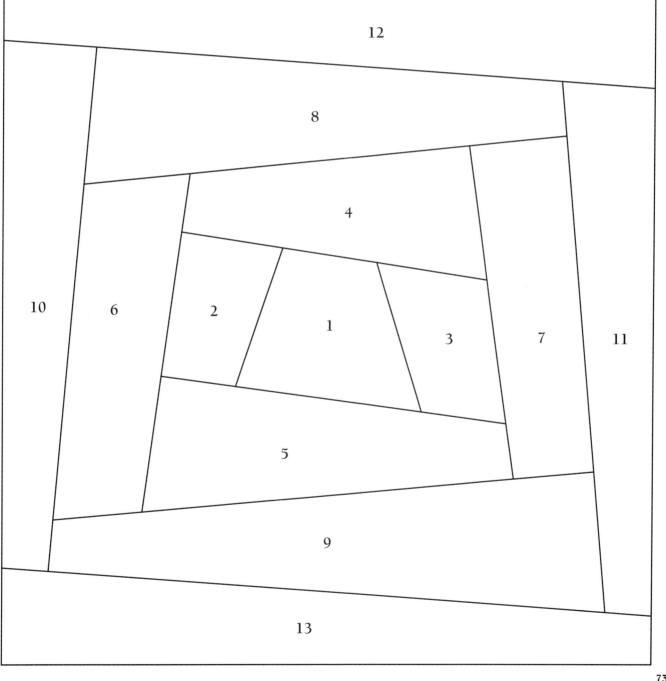

59

- (A) Feather Stitch
- (B) Cretan Stitch
- (C) Straight Stitch
- (D) Herringbone Stitch
- (E) Maidenhair Stitch

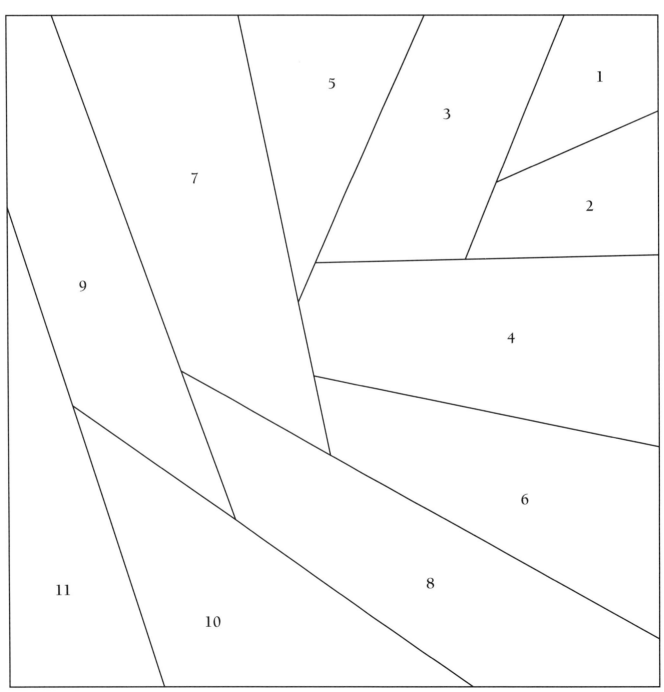

(A) Feather Stitch
(B) Cross Stitch
(C) Blanket Stitch

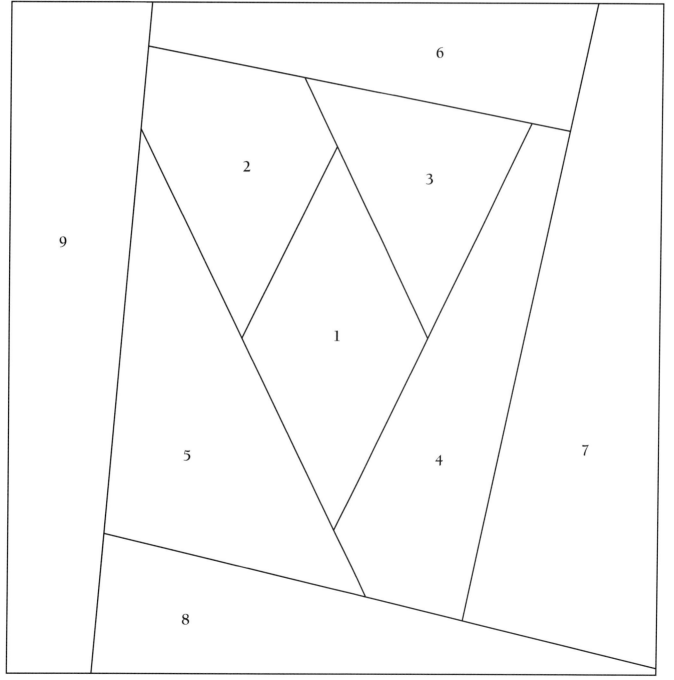

61

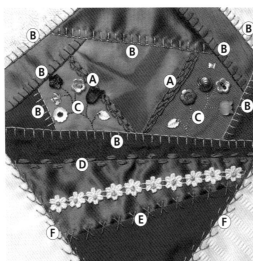

- (A) Chain Stitch (two rows)
- (B) Blanket Stitch
- (C) Backstitch
- (D) Running Stitch (silk ribbon)
- (E) Cross Stitch
- (F) Feather Stitch

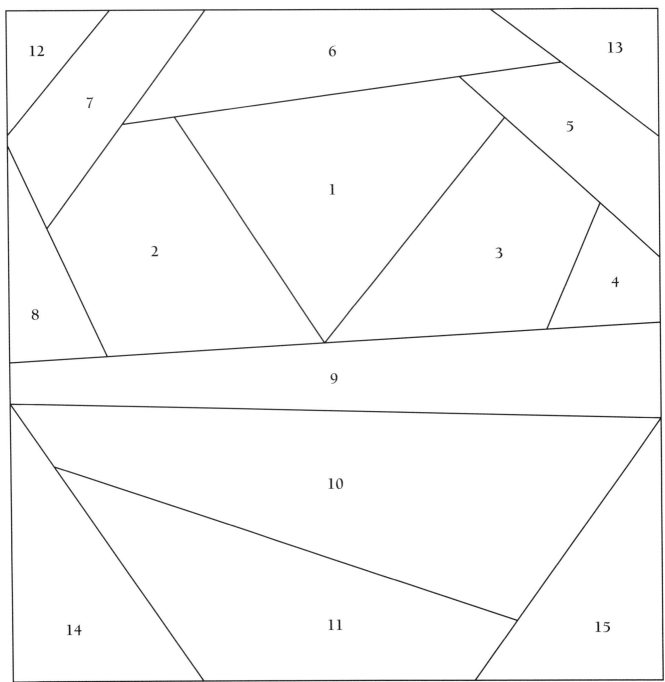

(A) Chain Stitch
(B) Feather stitch
(C) Chevron Stitch
(D) Wheat Ear Stitch
(E) Maidenhair Stitch
(F) Herringbone Stitch
(G) Running Stitch (to attach ribbon)

62

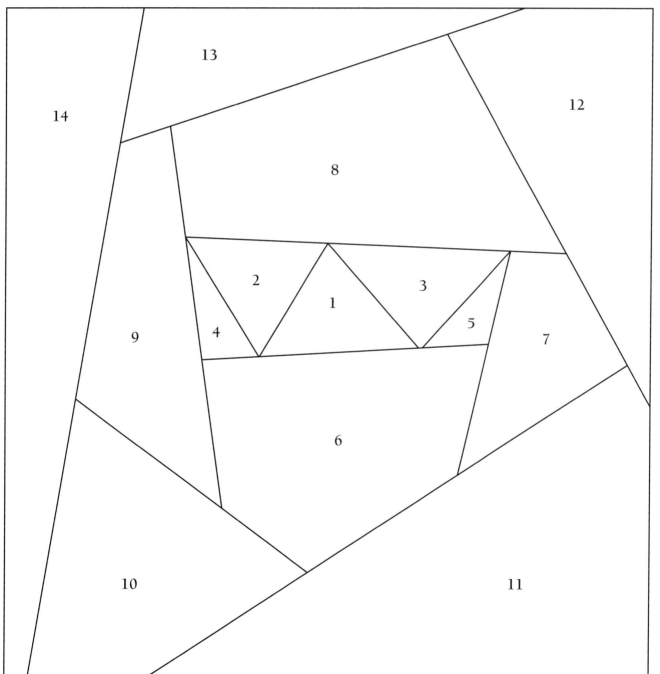

63

- (A) Blanket Stitch
- (B) Chain Stitch
- (C) Stem Stitch
- (D) Lazy Daisy
- (E) Colonial Knot
- (F) Fly Stitch
- (G) Maidenhair Stitch

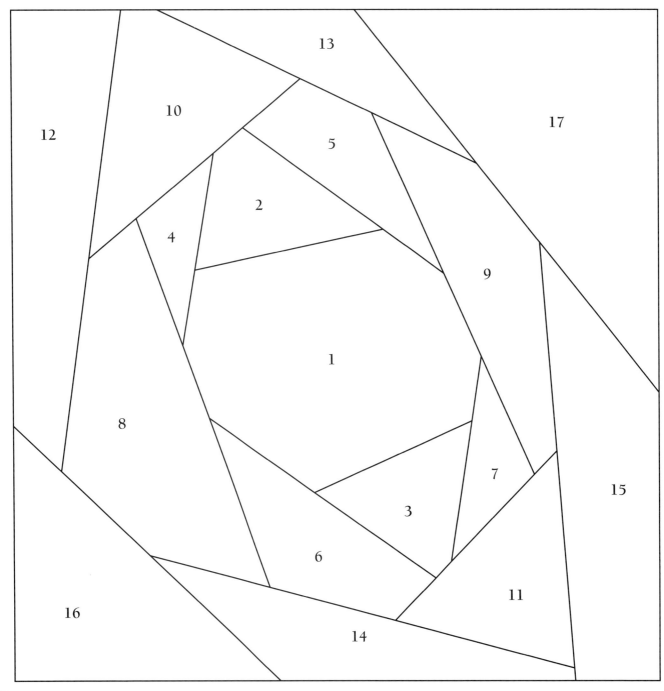

(A) Feather Stitch
(B) Maidenhair Stitch
(C) Wheat Ear Stitch
(D) Chevron Stitch
(E) Vandyke Stitch
(F) Lazy Daisy
(G) French Knot

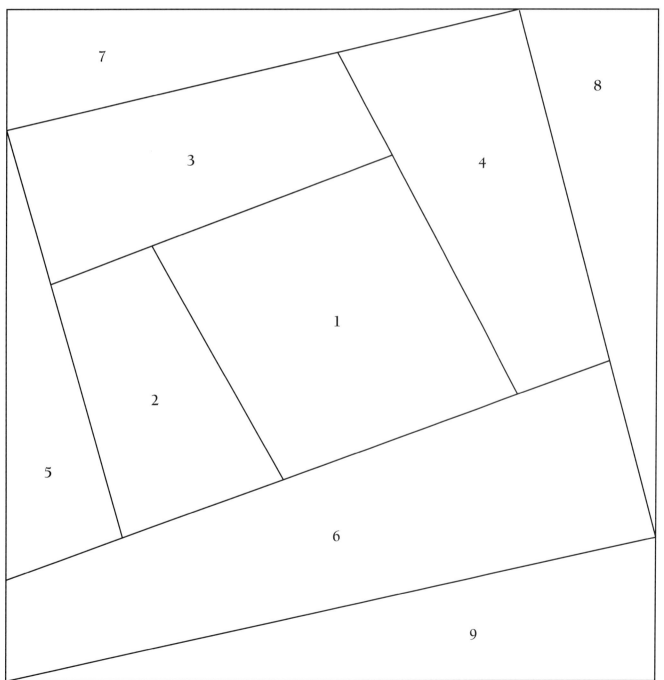

65

- (A) Blanket Stitch-closed
- (B) Chevron Stitch
- (C) Wheat Ear Stitch
- (D) Cross Stitch
- (E) Vandyke Stitch
- (F) Cretan Stitch
- (G) Feather Stitch
- (H) Fly Stitch
- (I) Chain Stitch (two rows)

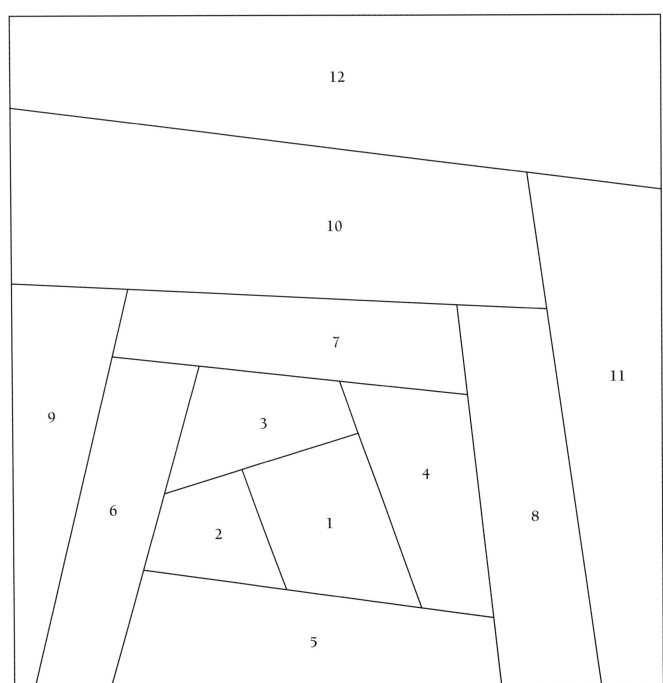

(A) Feather Stitch
(B) Wheat Ear Stitch
(C) Blanket Stitch
(D) Blanket Stitch-closed
(E) Vandyke Stitch
(F) Maidenhair Stitch

66

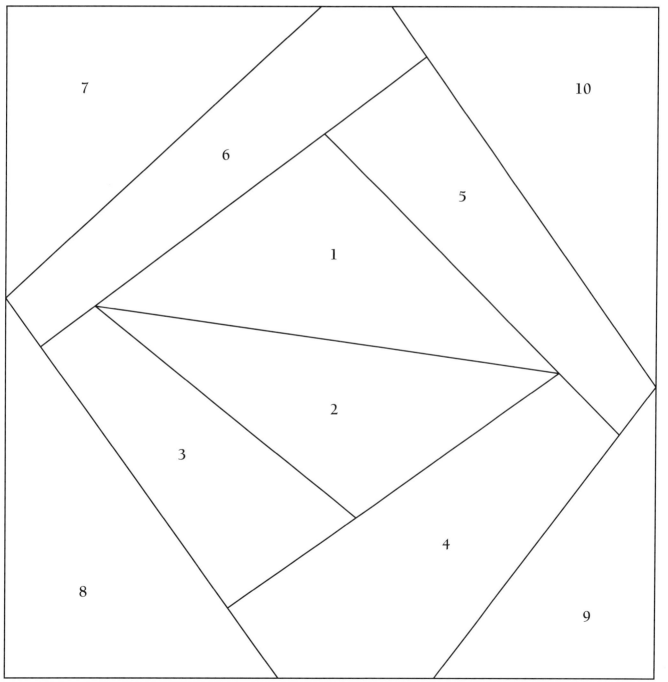

67

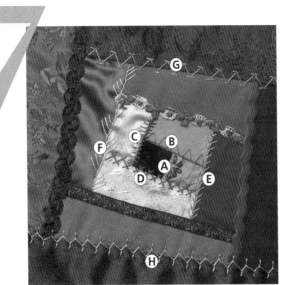

- (A) Lazy Daisy
- (B) Blanket Stitch-closed
- (C) Vandyke Stitch
- (D) Herringbone Stitch
- (E) Wheat Ear Stitch
- (F) Maidenhair Stitch
- (G) Chevron Stitch
- (H) Cretan Stitch

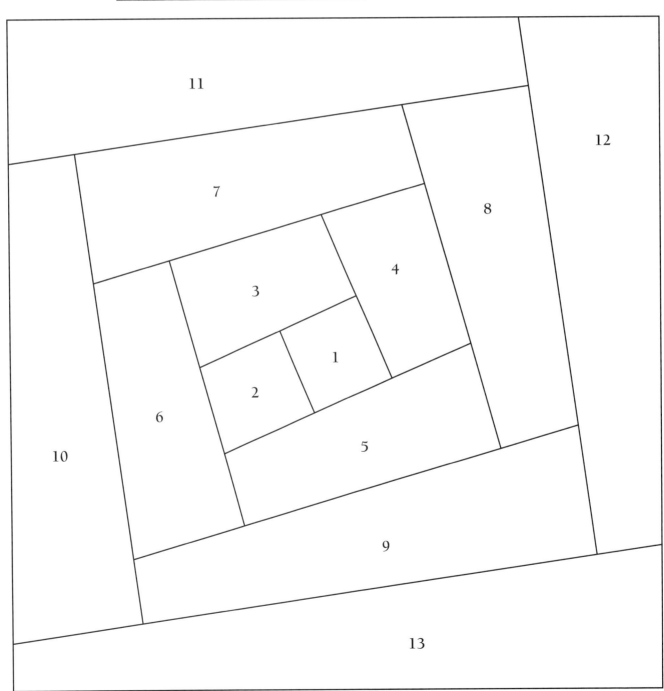

(A) Cross Stitch
(B) Chain Stitch
(C) Cretan Stitch
(D) Chevron Stitch
(E) Blanket Stitch-closed
(F) Blanket Stitch
(G) Fly Stitch
(H) Feather Stitch

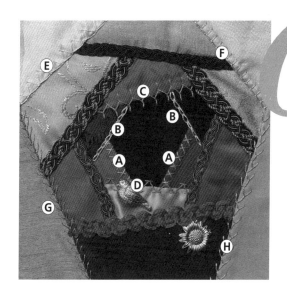

68

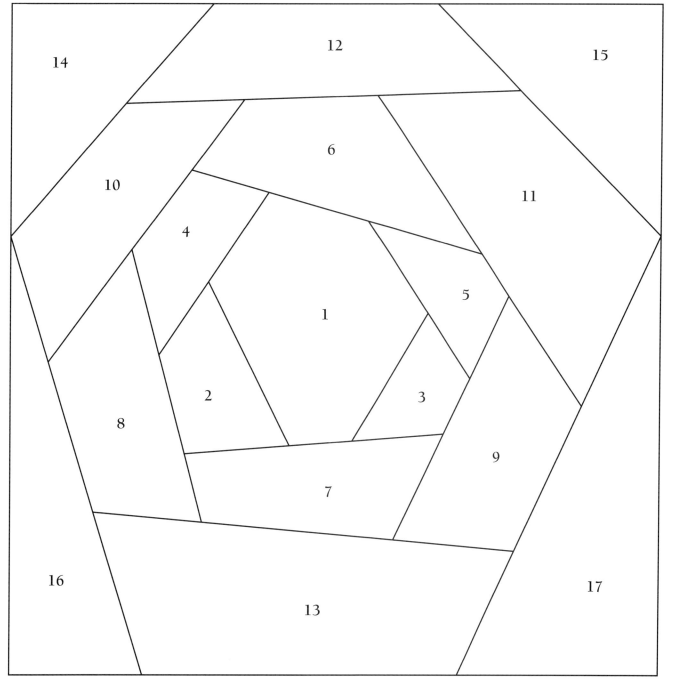

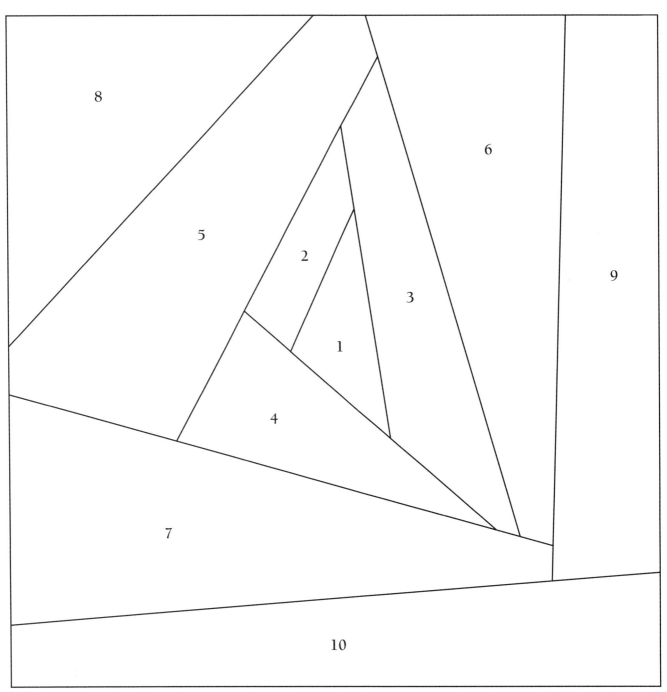

69

(A) Blanket Stitch
(B) Feather Stitch
(C) Cretan Stitch
(D) Wheat Ear Stitch
(E) Maidenhair Stitch
(F) Herringbone Stitch

(A) Blanket Stitch
(B) Chevron Stitch
(C) Vandyke Stitch
(D) Colonial Knot
(E) Chain Stitch
(F) Cretan Stitch
(G) Wheat Ear Stitch
(H) Herringbone Stitch
(I) Lazy Daisy
(J) Feather Stitch
(K) Maidenhair Stitch
(L) Stem Stitch
(M) Blanket Stitch-closed
(N) Cross Stitch

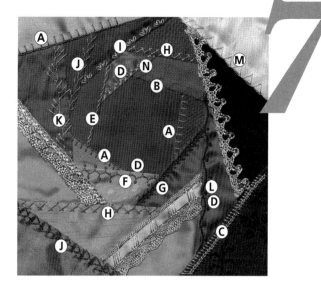

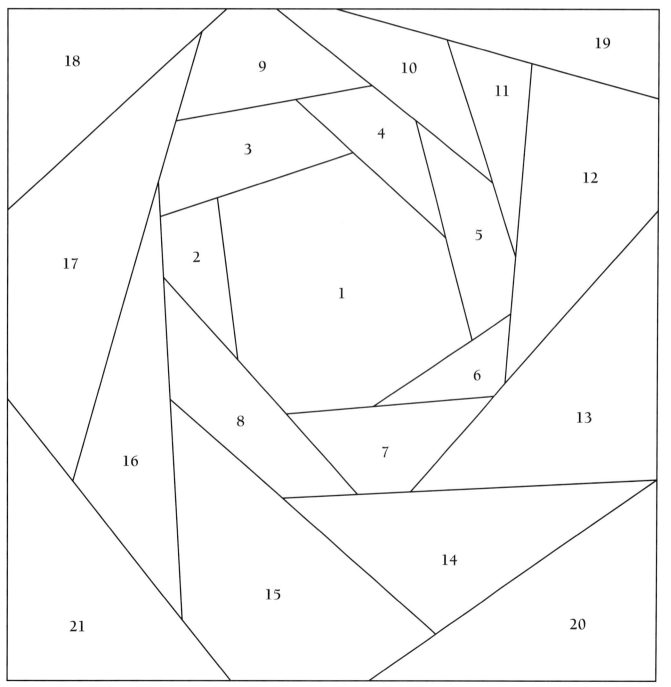

71

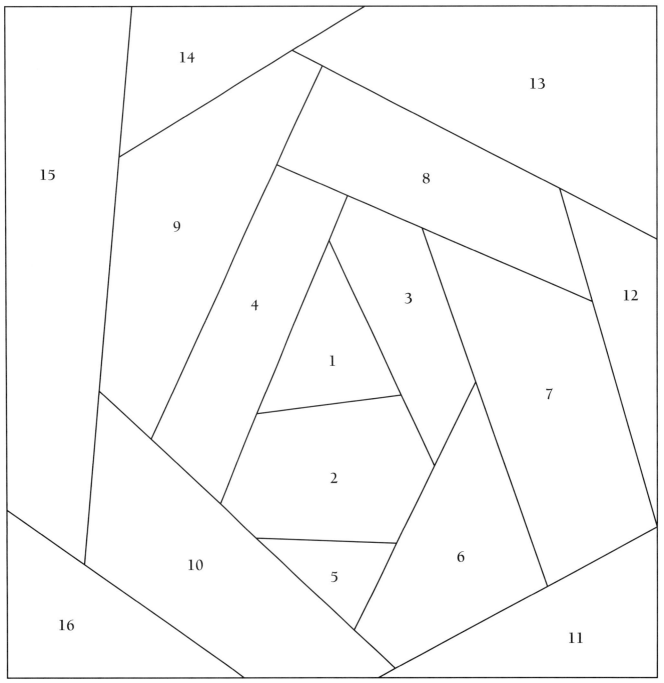

- (A) Chevron Stitch
- (B) Wheat Ear Stitch
- (C) Vandyke Stitch
- (D) Blanket Stitch
- (E) Feather Stitch
- (F) Cretan Stitch
- (G) Herringbone Stitch
- (H) Chain Stitch
- (I) Stem Stitch
- (J) Lazy Daisy

A Fly Stitch
B Chain Stitch (two rows)
C Wheat Ear Stitch
D Feather Stitch
E Blanket Stitch
F Colonial Knot
G Herringbone Stitch
H Lazy Daisy
I Blanket Stitch-closed
J Cretan Stitch

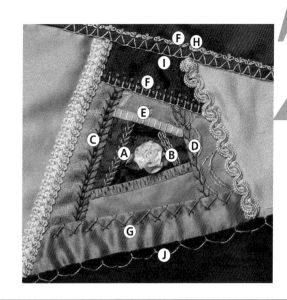

72

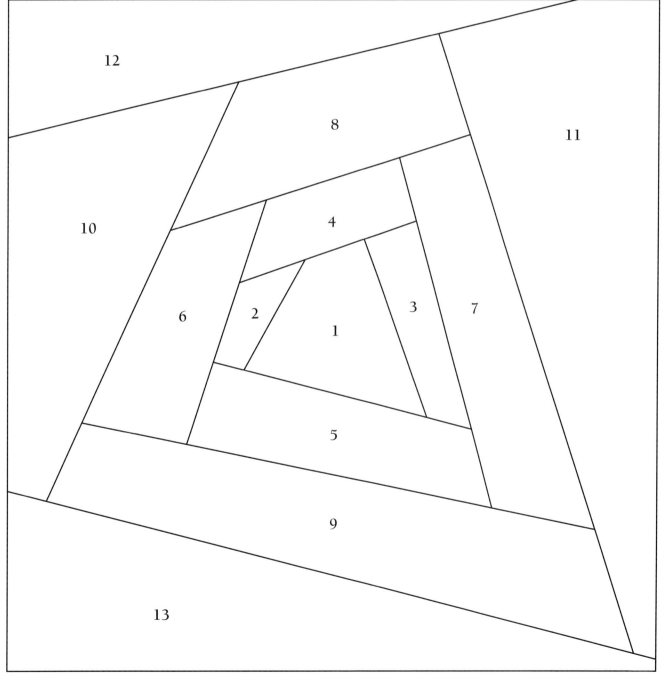

73

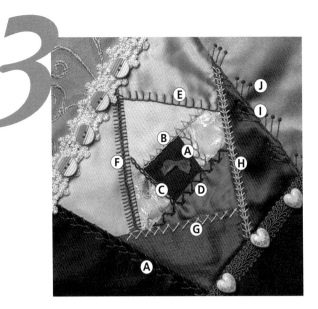

- (A) Feather Stitch
- (B) Blanket Stitch-closed
- (C) Chain Stitch
- (D) Chevron Stitch
- (E) Blanket Stitch
- (F) Vandyke Stitch
- (G) Herringbone Stitch
- (H) Wheat Ear Stitch
- (I) Maidenhair Stitch
- (J) Colonial Knot

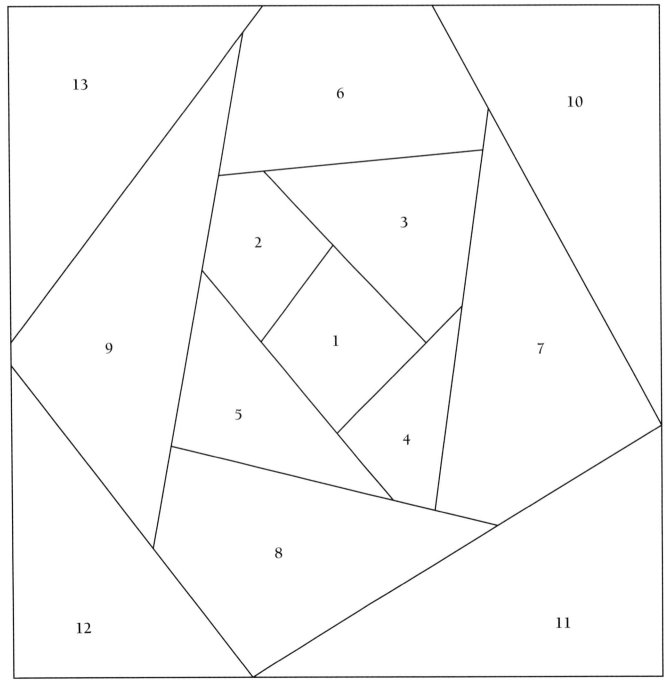

A Wheat Ear Stitch
B Chain Stitch
C Lazy Daisy
D Cretan Stitch
E Colonial Knot
F Chevron Stitch
G Stem Stitch
H Herringbone Stitch

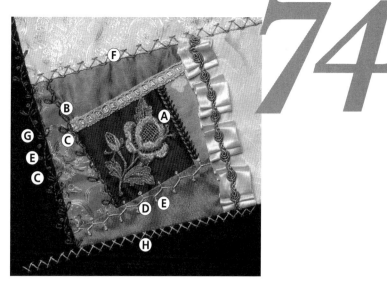

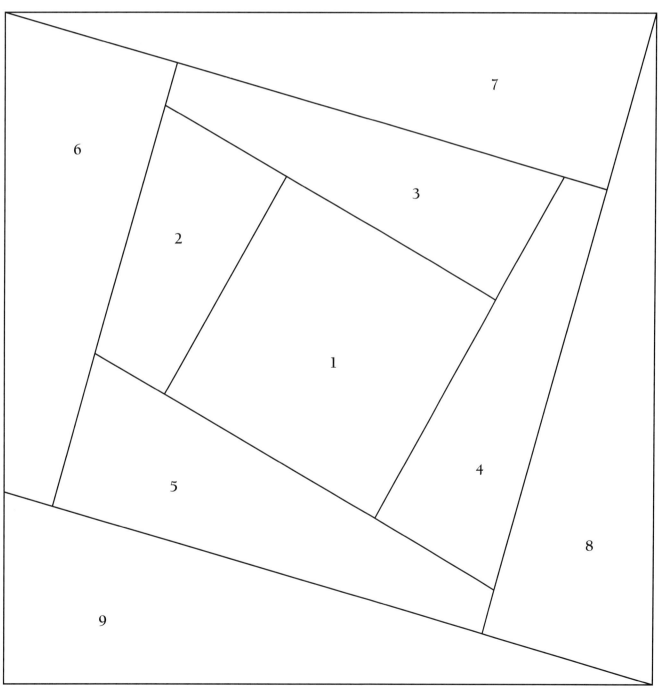

75

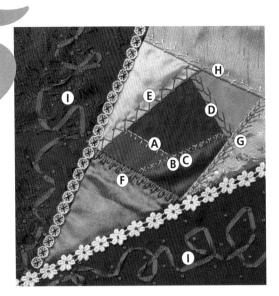

(A) Blanket Stitch
(B) Cross Stitch
(C) Colonial Knot
(D) Feather Stitch
(E) Chevron Stitch
(F) Lazy Daisy
(G) Fly Stitch
(H) Cretan Stitch
(I) Silk ribbon (attached with beads)

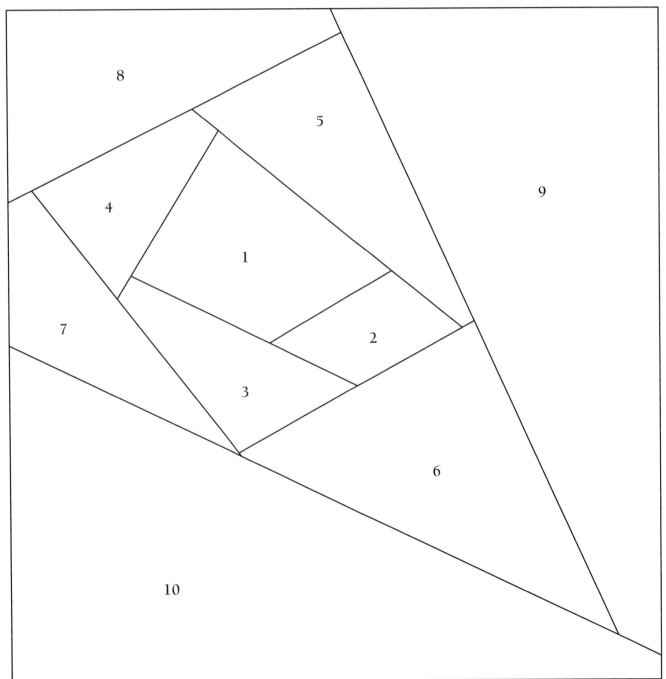

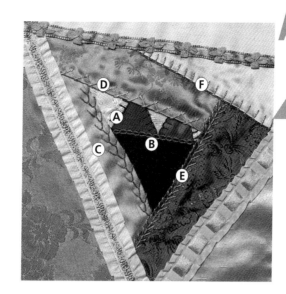

A) Blanket Stitch
B) Chain Stitch
C) Feather Stitch
D) Herringbone Stitch
E) Fly Stitch
F) Blanket Stitch

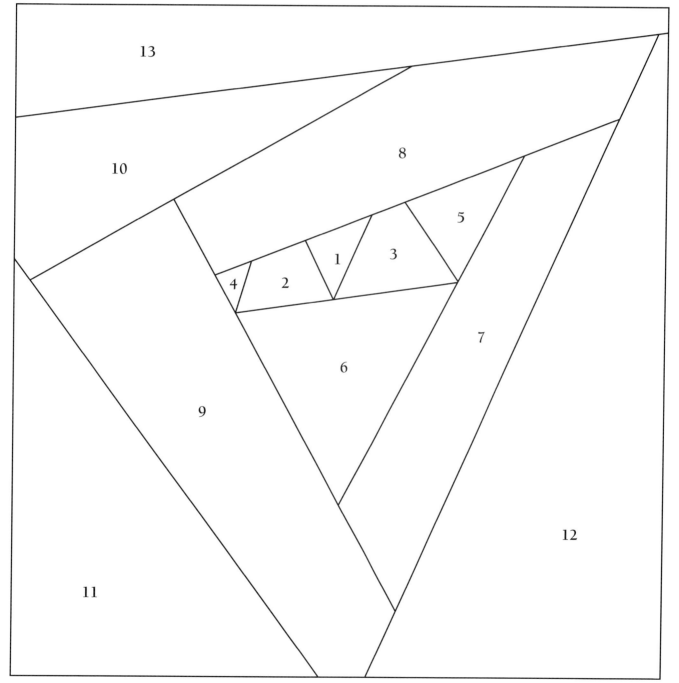

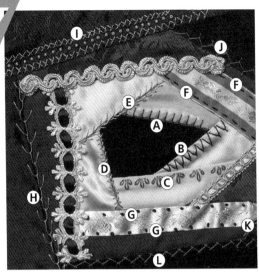

77

- (A) Blanket Stitch
- (B) Fly Stitch
- (C) Lazy Daisy
- (D) Vandyke Stitch
- (E) Wheat Ear Stitch
- (F) Running Stitch (to attach ribbon)
- (G) French Knot (to attach ribbon)
- (H) Feather Stitch
- (I) Cross Stitch (two rows with beads)
- (J) Cretan Stitch
- (K) Chain Stitch
- (L) Herringbone Stitch

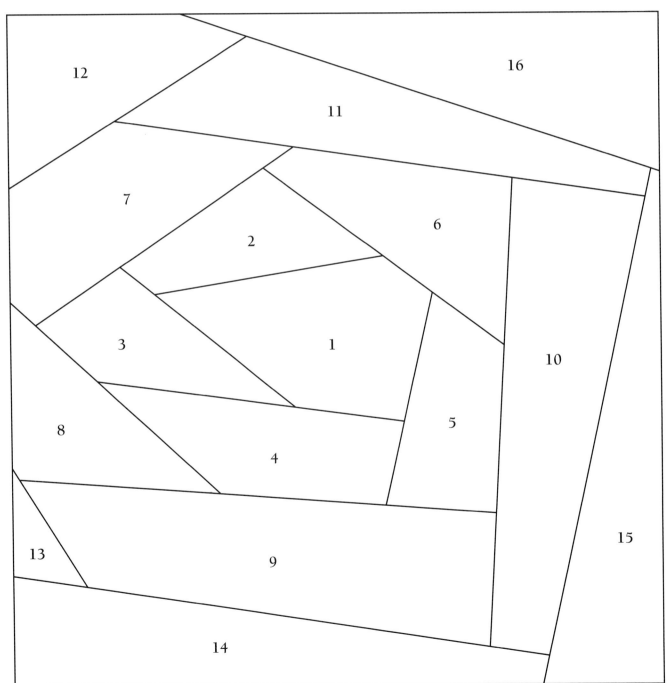

(A) Wheat Ear Stitch
(B) Vandyke Stitch
(C) Herringbone Stitch
(D) Cretan Stitch
(E) Feather Stitch
(F) Fly Stitch

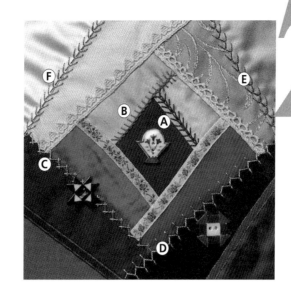

78

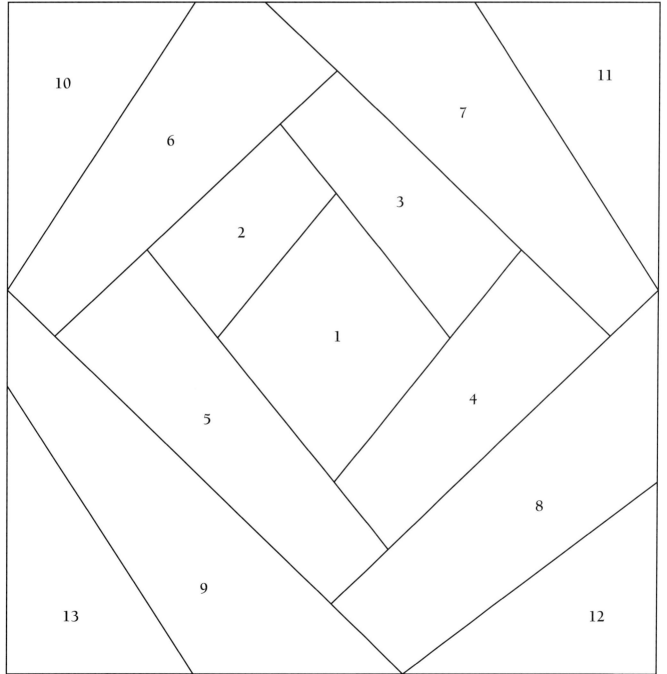

79

(A) Blanket Stitch
(B) Blanket Stitch-closed
(C) Fly Stitch
(D) Cross Stitch
(E) Chevron Stitch
(F) Feather Stitch
(G) Chain Stitch (three rows)
(H) Stem Stitch
(I) Lazy Daisy

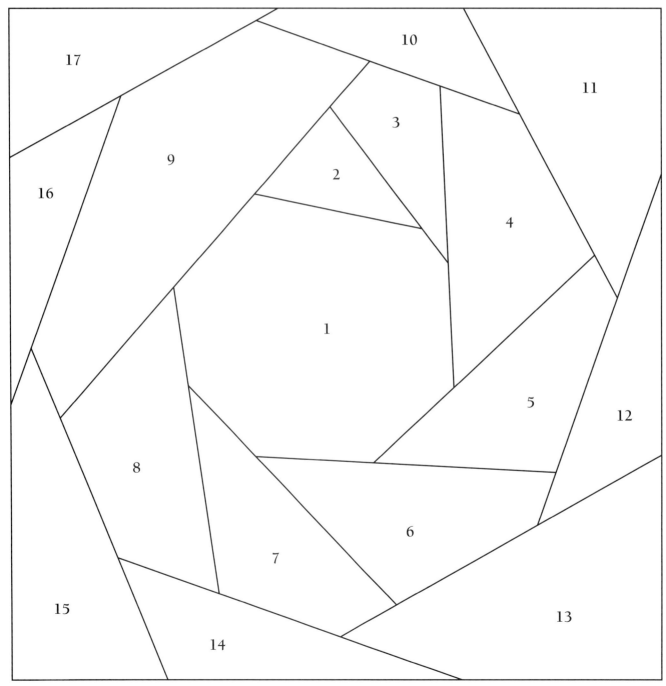

(A) Blanket Stitch
(B) Chevron Stitch
(C) Feather Stitch
(D) Cretan Stitch
(E) Wheat Ear Stitch

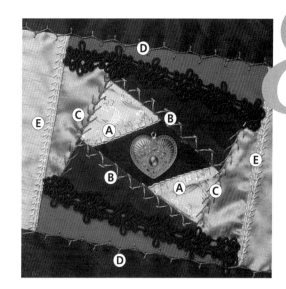

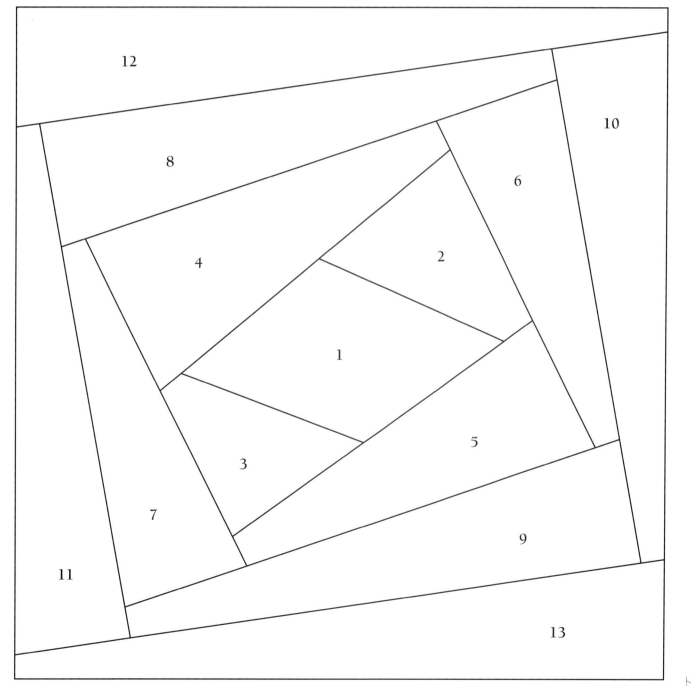

81

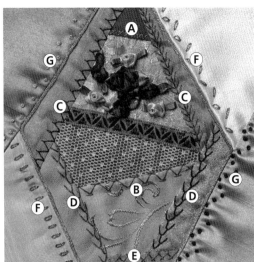

(A) Cross Stitch
(B) Chevron Stitch
(C) Fly Stitch
(D) Feather Stitch
(E) Herringbone Stitch
(F) Lazy Daisy
(G) Colonial Knot

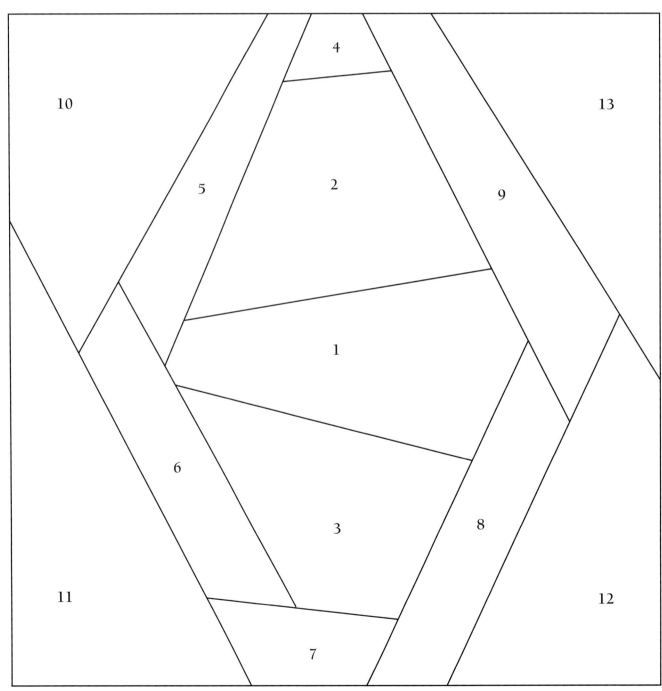

(A) Fly Stitch
(B) Maidenhair Stitch
(C) Cretan Stitch
(D) Feather Stitch

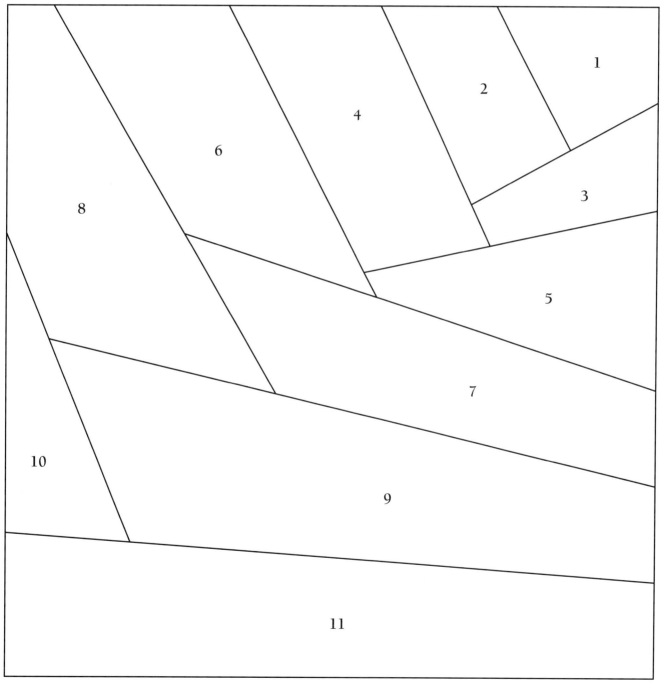

83

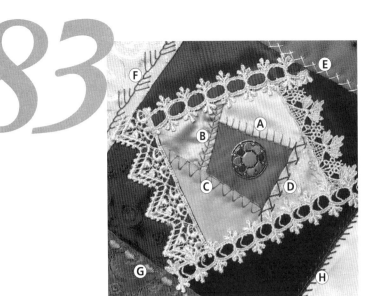

(A) Blanket Stitch
(B) Fly Stitch
(C) Blanket Stitch-closed
(D) Chevron Stitch
(E) Herringbone Stitch
(F) Maidenhair Stitch
(G) Satin Stitch
(H) Wheat Ear Stitch

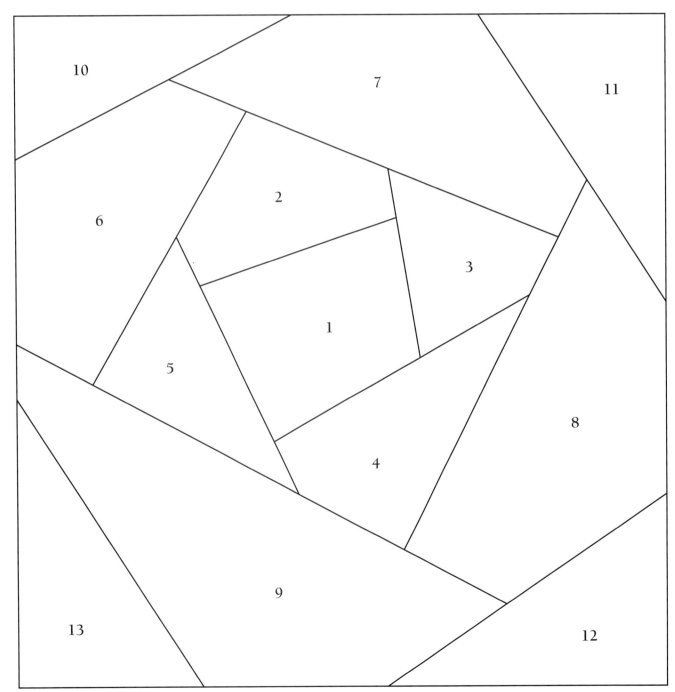

(A) Herringbone Stitch
(B) Chevron Stitch
(C) Lazy Daisy
(D) Blanket Stitch
(E) Feather Stitch
(F) Wheat Ear Stitch
(G) Vandyke Stitch

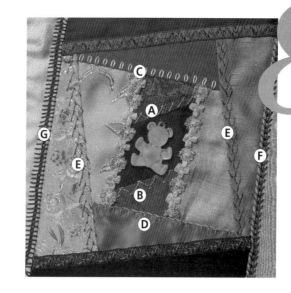

84

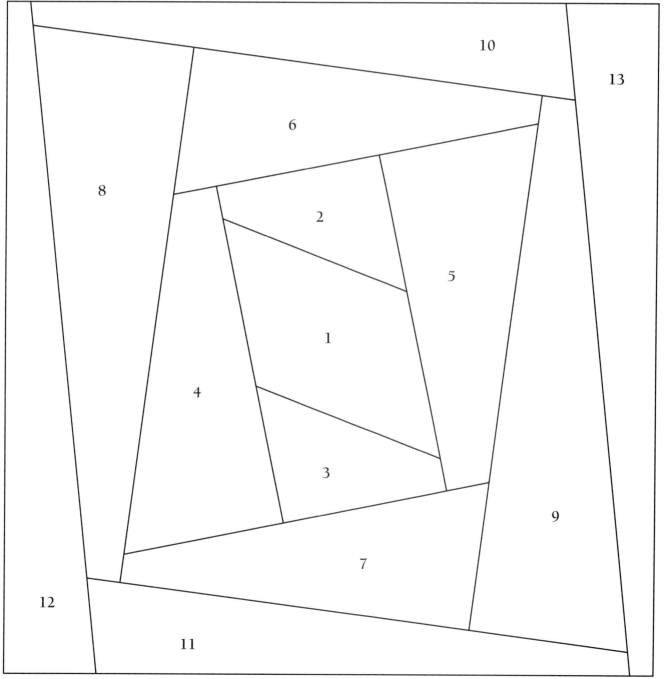

85

(A) Chevron Stitch
(B) Feather Stitch
(C) Herringbone Stitch
(D) Blanket Stitch
(E) Vandyke Stitch
(F) Colonial Knot (to attach lace)
(G) Chain Stitch
(H) Fly Stitch
(I) Wheat Ear Stitch
(J) Cretan Stitch

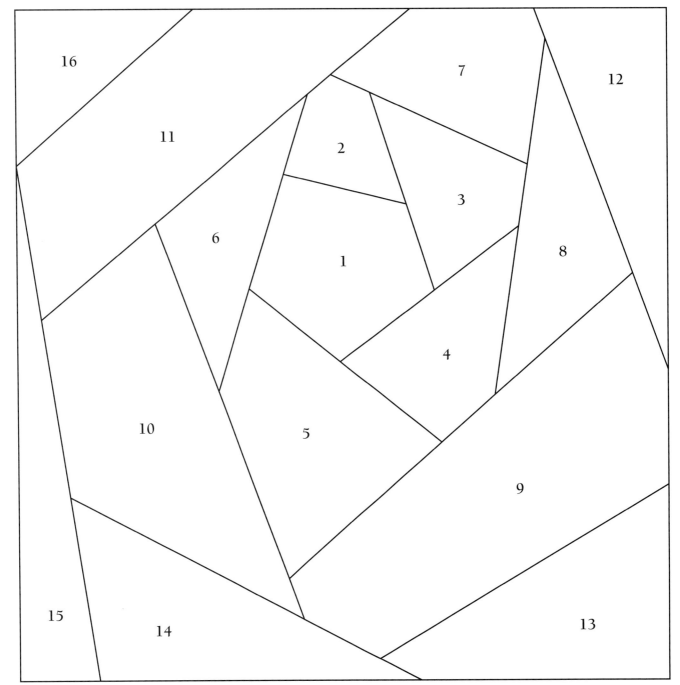

(A) Chain Stitch
(B) Wheat Ear Stitch
(C) Herringbone Stitch
(D) Feather Stitch
(E) Colonial Knot
(F) Fly Stitch
(G) Blanket Stitch
(H) Lace attached with beads

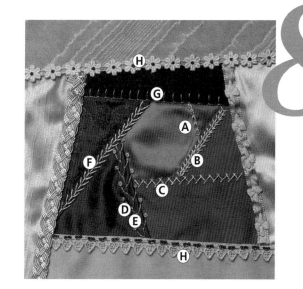

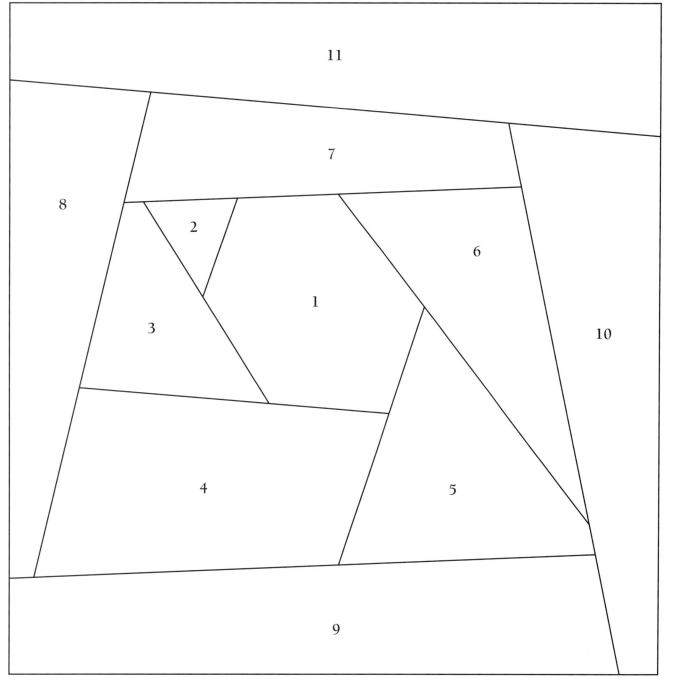

87

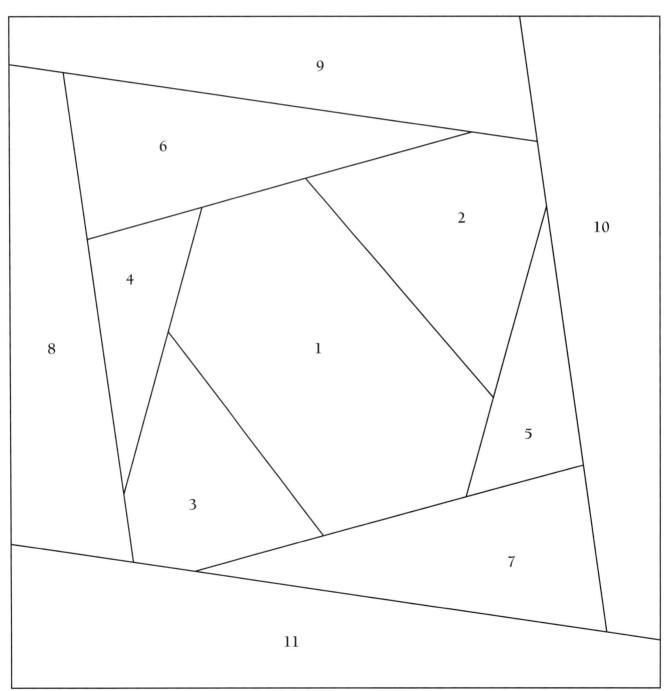

- (A) Straight Stitch
- (B) Lazy Daisy
- (C) Colonial Knot
- (D) Maidenhair Stitch (with beads)
- (E) Wheat Ear Stitch
- (F) Vandyke Stitch
- (G) Feather Stitch
- (H) Blanket Stitch
- (I) Blanket Stitch-closed
- (J) French Knot
- (K) Herringbone Stitch
- (L) Chevron Stitch

A Chain Stitch
B Lazy Daisy
C French Knot
D Cretan Stitch
E Fly Stitch
F Chevron Stitch
G Vandyke Stitch
H Feather Stitch
I Colonial Knot (silk ribbon)
J Wheat Ear Stitch
K Blanket Stitch-closed
L Maidenhair Stitch

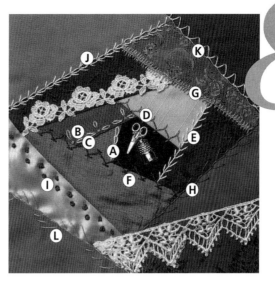

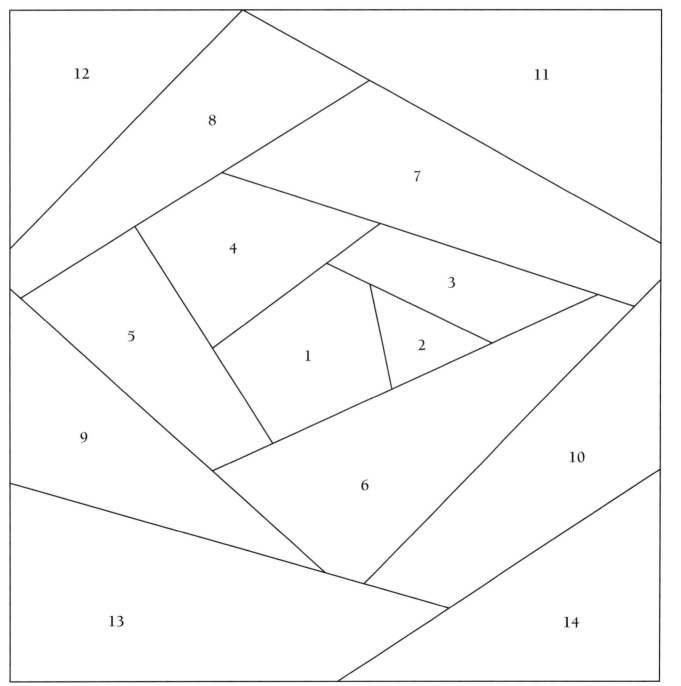

89

(A) Fly Stitch
(B) Vandyke Stitch
(C) Feather Stitch
(D) Blanket Stitch
(E) Stem Stitch
(F) French Knot

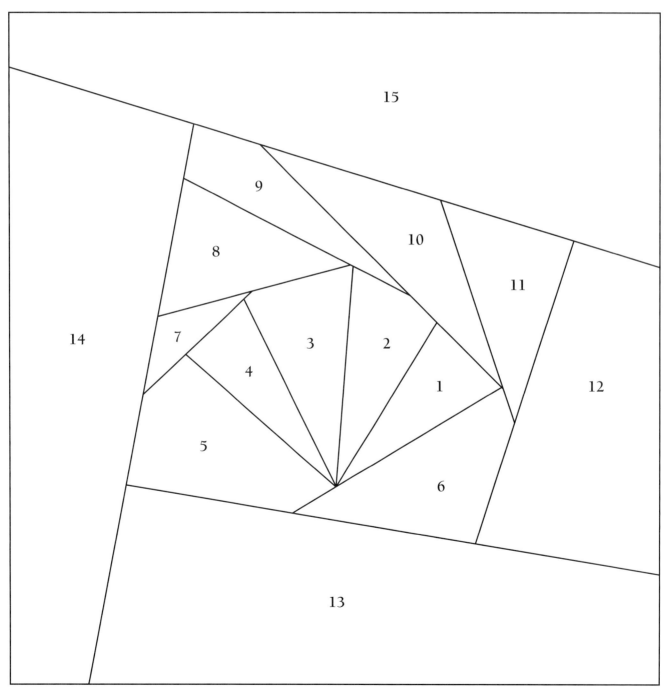

- (A) Blanket Stitch
- (B) Blanket Stitch-closed
- (C) Chain Stitch (two rows)
- (D) Fly Stitch
- (E) Satin Stitch
- (F) Wheat Ear Stitch
- (G) Cross Stitch
- (H) Cretan Stitch
- (I) Stem Stitch
- (J) Colonial Knot (silk ribbon)
- (K) Lazy Daisy
- (L) Running Stitch (silk ribbon)
- (M) Chain Stitch
- (N) Chevron Stitch

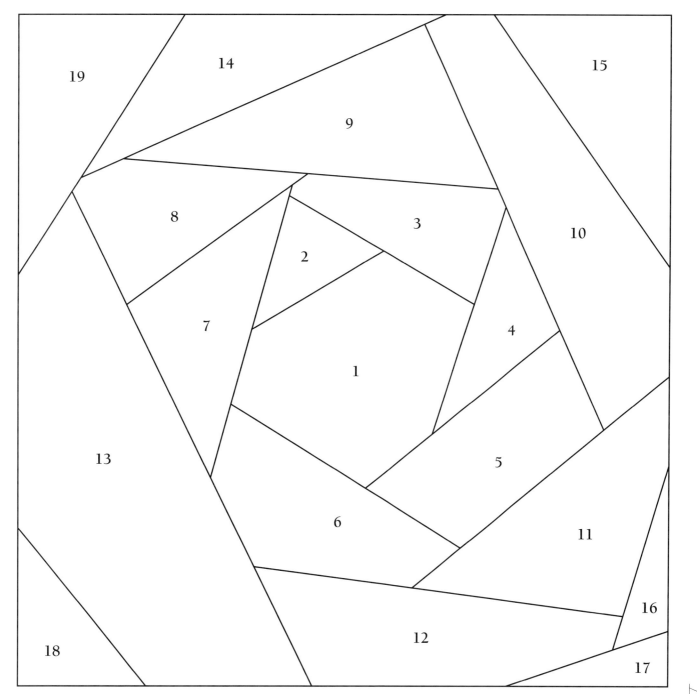

91

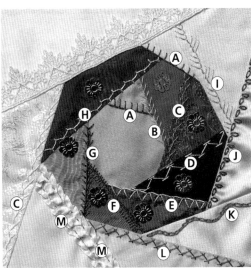

(A) Blanket Stitch
(B) Fly Stitch
(C) Feather Stitch
(D) Chevron Stitch
(E) Blanket Stitch-closed
(F) Vandyke Stitch
(G) Wheat Ear Stitch
(H) Cretan Stitch
(I) Maidenhair Stitch
(J) Lazy Daisy
(K) Chain Stitch
(L) Herringbone Stitch
(M) Running Stitch (to attach ribbon)

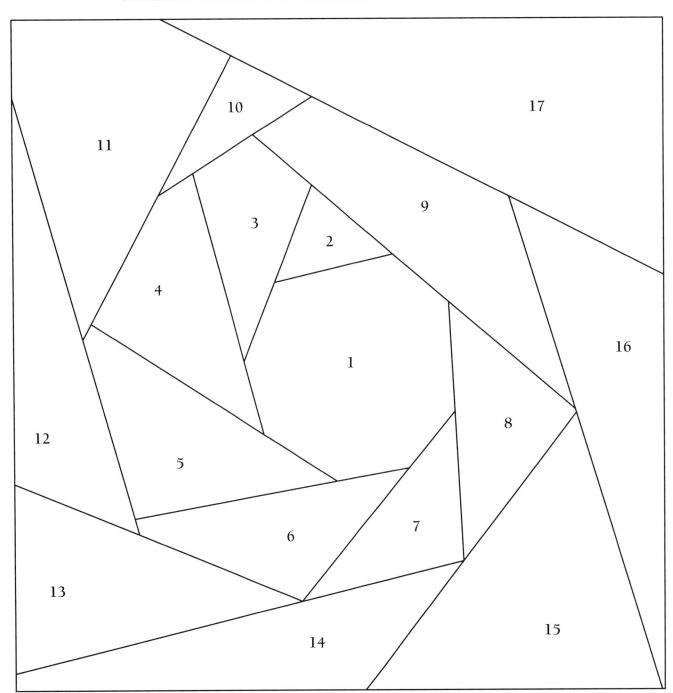

(A) Stem Stitch (outline of lace flowers)
(B) Fly Stitch
(C) Feather Stitch
(D) Chevron Stitch
(E) Lazy Daisy
(F) Maidenhair Stitch

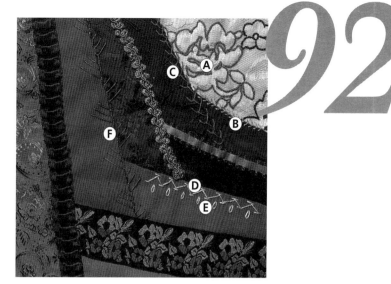

92

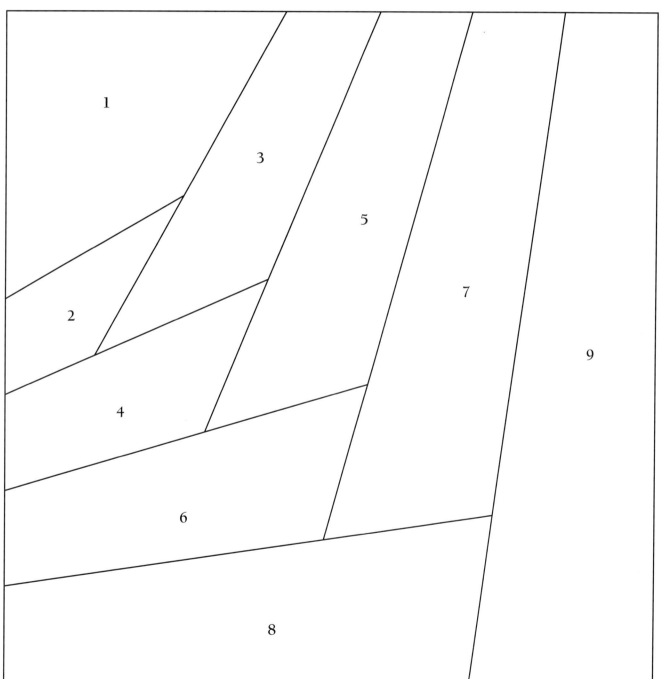

93

- (A) Chain Stitch
- (B) Feather Stitch
- (C) Stem Stitch
- (D) Blanket Stitch
- (E) Chevron Stitch
- (F) Wheat Ear Stitch
- (G) Cross Stitch
- (H) Blanket Stitch-closed
- (I) Vandyke Stitch
- (J) Herringbone Stitch

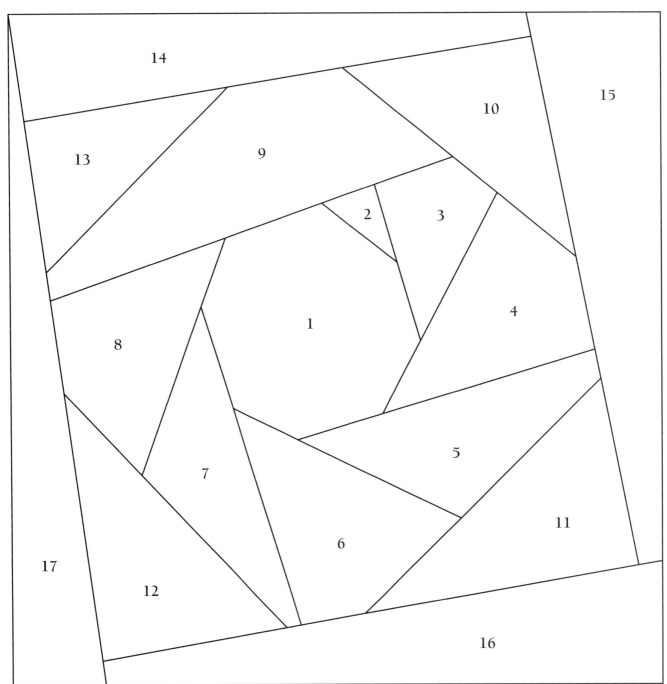

- (A) Fly Stitch
- (B) Chevron Stitch
- (C) Feather Stitch
- (D) Lazy Daisy
- (E) Feather Stitch

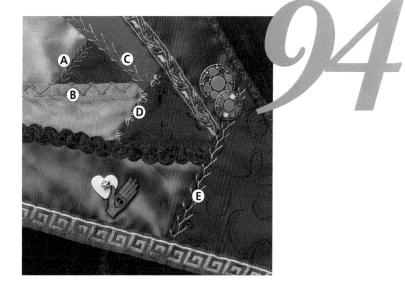

94

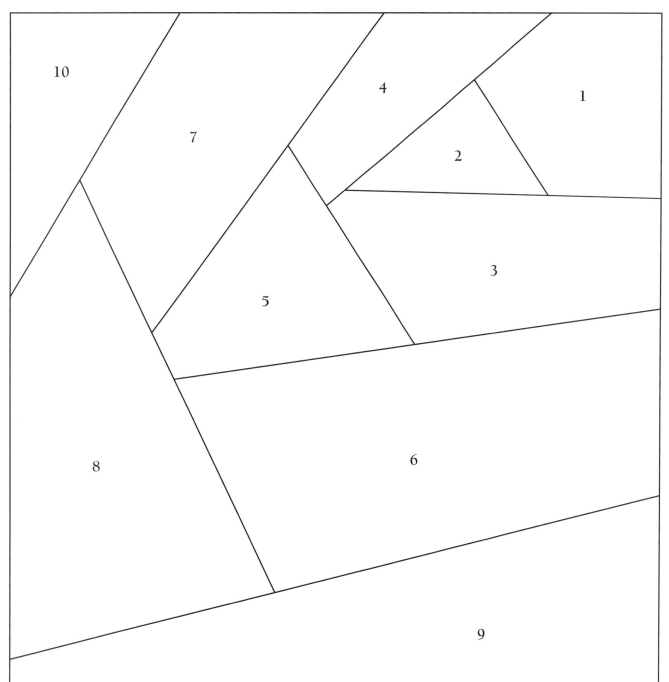

95

(A) Chevron Stitch
(B) Herringbone Stitch
(C) Feather Stitch
(D) Blanket Stitch
(E) Maidenhair Stitch
(F) Fly Stitch

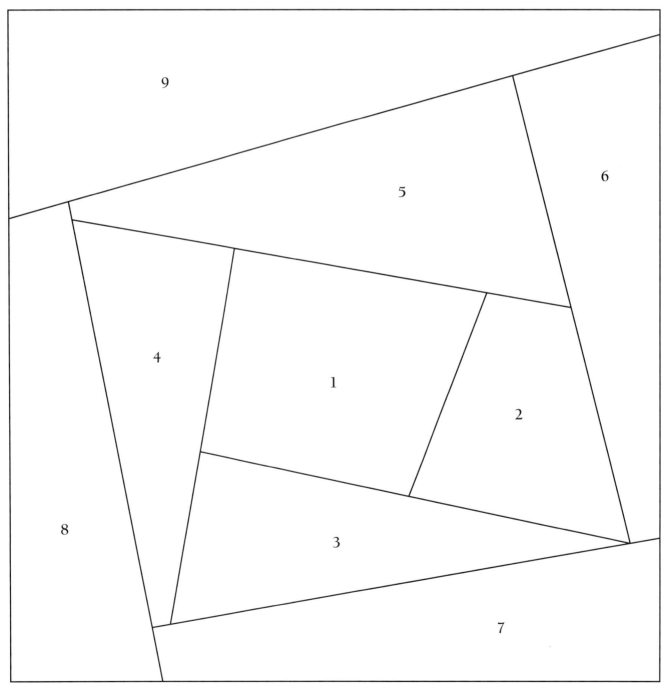

- (A) Colonial Knot
- (B) Chain Stitch
- (C) Cretan Stitch
- (D) Feather Stitch
- (E) Wheat Ear Stitch
- (F) Blanket Stitch
- (G) Lazy Daisy
- (H) Chevron Stitch
- (I) Maidenhair Stitch
- (J) Vandyke Stitch

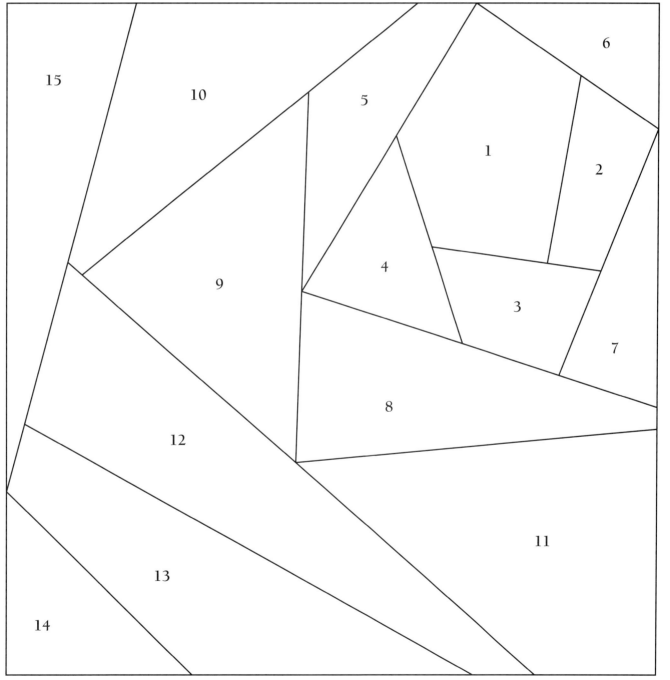

97

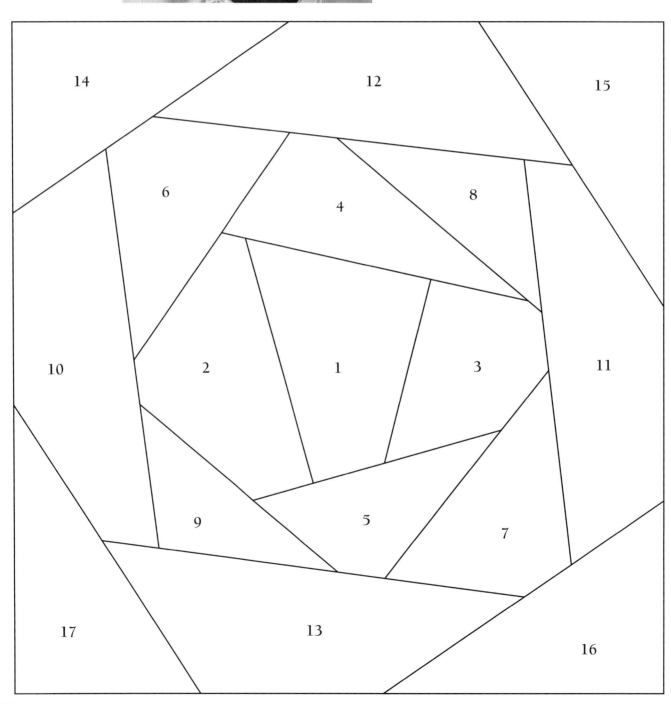

- (A) Feather Stitch
- (B) Chevron Stitch
- (C) Wheat Ear Stitch
- (D) Vandyke Stitch
- (E) Blanket Stitch-closed
- (F) Herringbone Stitch

(A) Blanket Stitch-closed
(B) Herringbone Stitch
(C) Maidenhair Stitch
(D) Feather Stitch

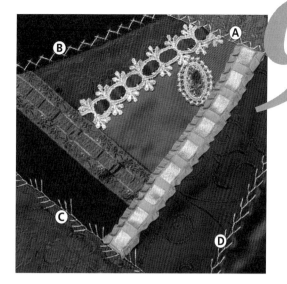

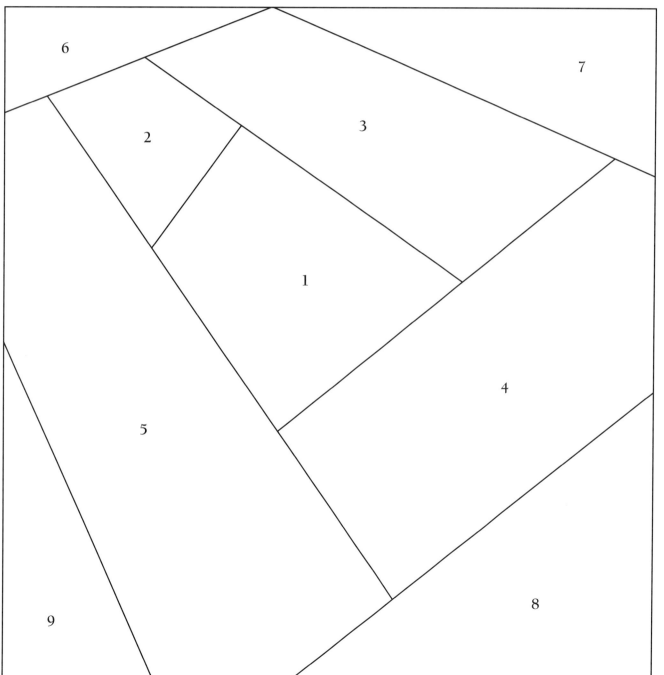

(A) Vandyke Stitch
(B) Fly Stitch
(C) Herringbone Stitch
(D) Wheat Ear Stitch
(E) Blanket Stitch
(F) Feather Stitch

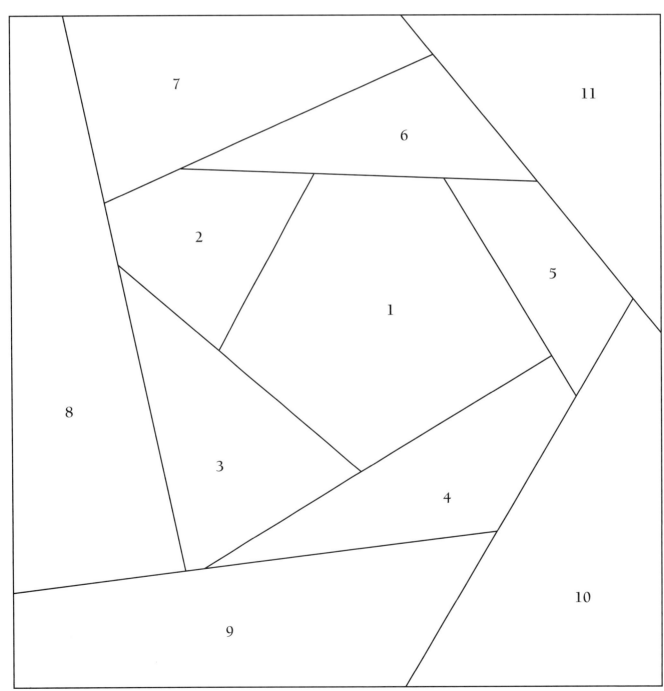

(A) Maidenhair Stitch (with beads)

(B) Feather Stitch (with beads)

(C) Cretan Stitch

(D) Lazy Daisy

(E) Wheat Ear Stitch

(F) Fly Stitch

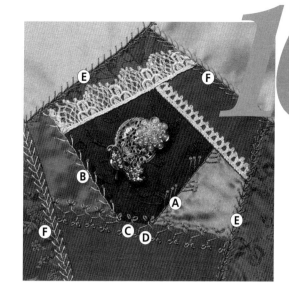

100

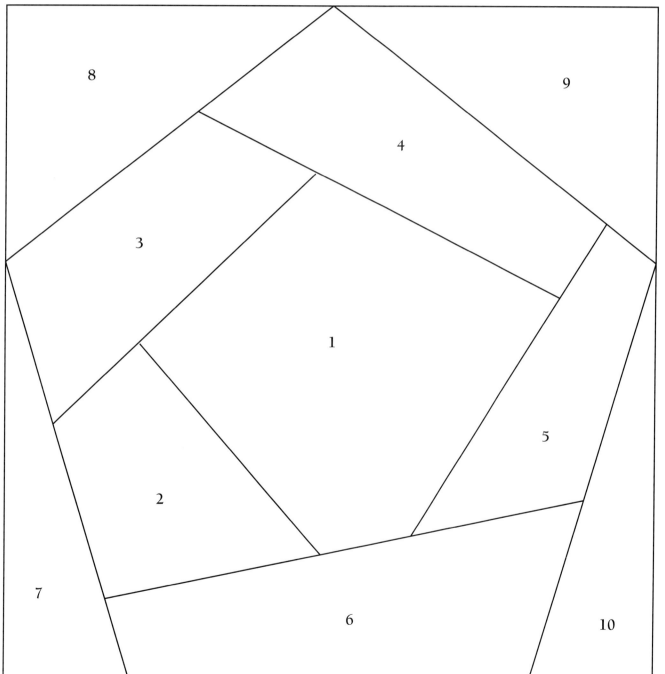

101

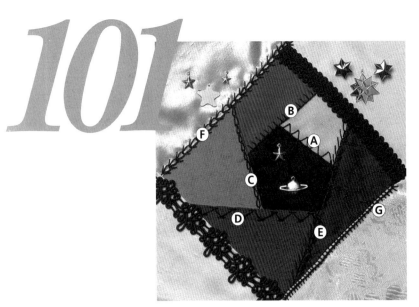

(A) Blanket Stitch-closed
(B) Blanket Stitch
(C) Chain Stitch
(D) Chevron Stitch
(E) Fly Stitch
(F) Wheat Ear Stitch
(G) Vandyke Stitch

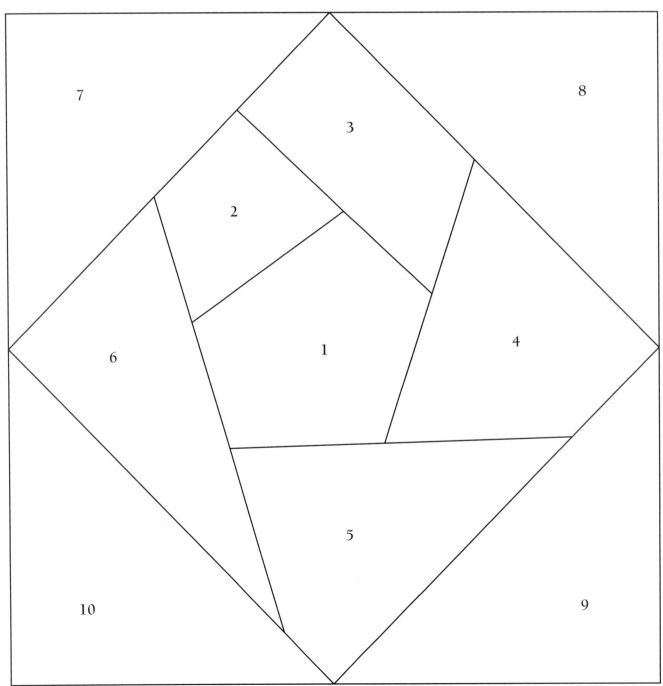